He Is Just That into You

He Is Just That into You

Stories of a Faithful God who Pursues, Engages,

and has No Fear of Commitment

Elisabeth K. Corcoran

Pleasant Word (a division of WinePress Publishing, PO Box 428, Enumclaw, WA 98022) functions only as book publisher. As such, the ultimate design, content, editorial accuracy, and views expressed or implied in this work are those of the author.

ISBN 13: 978-1-4141-1487-3
ISBN 10: 1-4141-1487-7
Library of Congress Catalog Card Number: 2009904998

Contents

Foreword

WHEN I SAT down to write this collection of stories…let me rephrase, when it came pouring out of me…I did not have a theme in mind. But as I look back a year later at what I've pulled together, I can't help but think of something I heard recently. You can look upon writing as the chance to tell the world the one thing you believe the most about life. I've been ending each talk in the same fashion for the past eight years, and I dare say that as long as I am granted the privilege to write, my *one thing* will remain the same. So in a sentence, this is what I believe the most in the whole world that I would give anything to tell the whole world: God loves me and God loves you; so much that He could only show it through the outrageously generous act of allowing His Son to die and come back to life for me and for you…it's that kind of big, crazy, perfect love. Okay, long sentence. But I believe it down into my bones. It's what my life is about. And it's what this book is essentially about as well.

Since the dawn of time, the story goes…boy meets girl, boy or girl does something that ticks off the other, they either break up and look elsewhere for supposed greener pastures, or hang on to each other through thick and thin.

Women are looking for something that will last. There's almost no getting around it…we are basically programmed as little girls to seek out our Prince Charming. That's a lot of pressure on the men of the world. We look for one to meet all the needs we've got pent up and then when they don't...or better put, when they *can't*, because they weren't created to...we either carry on to our girlfriends, cry about it, or just plain bail.

But what if the Love that we're really looking for actually can last a lifetime, and then some? And what if that Love won't be found in a guy?

In these pages, you will find a collection of stories from one woman's life, *my life*, of a faithful God who pursues, engages, and has no fear of commitment. Stories of ways He's showed up for me time and time again, of ways He's met those needs, trivial or life-changing. Worldly love can come and go, ebb and flow; male-female relationships—even committed, healthy, married ones—will go through rocky times, and can leave you feeling all alone.

But there is a Love that will not let you down, that will not walk away, that will not find someone else more appealing, that will be a part of your everyday life, and will have no problem laying His life down for you, loving you fully for the rest of your days.

I hope in the reflections I've made on my journey so far, you are encouraged in the journey you're on...to lift your gaze just above the dailyness of life and reach out for the hand of God who wants to faithfully love you, pursue you, engage you, and commit to you. There are blessings and nudges and answers to prayer and people who drop into your life and circumstances that shift ever so slightly and miracles that blow you away and you realize, hopefully, that God was in each one of those moments. We could all use more stories like that. Stories that remind us He's just a breath away. Stories that remind us He loves us more than we can even imagine. Stories that each one of us are living out every single day.

One final note. Whether you find yourself gratefully in a committed married relationship that is healthy, fulfilling, and thriving; in a relationship that's not quite there or nowhere near; or happily or longingly single, I think we all have one thing in common. We are looking for a Big Love that will never let us go. We are. We were created for that Love. But if you're anything like me, and I'm kind of banking on it, then sometimes, what you're looking for is that Big Love in human form.

But allow me to let you in on a little secret. That Big Love doesn't come in human form. And not because men are bad or lacking, by any means, but because human beings don't always love well and gloriously and romantically. So the reality is this: he, whoever your *he* is, may not always be all that into you. (But then again, maybe he is, and be grateful.) But the deep good news: capital letter He *is* just that into you. All the time. For the rest of eternity. No matter what.

I know that skin and bones is sometimes what you're looking for. But guess what? God knows that about us, too. He can meet us in that place. He can heal us in that place. He can fill the deep need of that place. To help us cease the striving and be so filled up with His perfect love for us that comes from simply abiding. And it comes. In fits and starts, sometimes. Abundantly at other times. But it comes. Take a look at my stories and then take a look at yours. Just look. Just hold on. Just listen. Just wait. The Love will come....the Love is right there.

Acknowledgments

THEY SAY THE process of writing a book is not an isolated one, and I agree. However, though my friends and family were nothing short of prayerfully supportive and encouraging, this particular project flowed primarily out of the healing relationship between my Heavenly Father and me. This is *my* testament. These stories point to the fact… yes, *the fact*…that what I hold to be true—that God is faithful, aware, and intimate…*is* true—and don't even get me started on how full of love He is. Oh wait, that's what this entire book is about…

I

Once upon a time, there was a girl who...

...looked inside and heard God...

Chapter 1

B-E-T-H Stands for What?

MY FOURTH-GRADE SON came home from school with a project he had worked on. Sometime during the first week of school, his teacher had asked the class to write their names vertically on a piece of paper. Then they were to create an acrostic with the letters of their names.

This is what my son wrote:

J esus Lover
A ddition whiz
C areful
K eeper

(He said the "Keeper" was because he keeps his money, "like Dad, not like you, Mom.")

As you can imagine, tears immediately formed in my eyes when I saw that of all the "J" things in the world that my son could have called himself, let alone the first week at a new school when kids jockey for friendships and the hunt for status begins, he identified himself as a "Jesus Lover." I have a feeling Jesus was pretty proud of my little boy in that moment, even more than I was.

God nudged my heart on this…if I had to write an acrostic about myself in front of a group of strangers, would any of the letters in my name willingly point out my rank as a follower of Christ? Or would I be too cowardly, too faithless, to let anyone see that about me, to define myself by that fairly distinguishable quality? I know what I'd like to believe about myself, but I also know what I'm truly capable of. May "Jesus Lover" find its way into my self-description. And into yours as well.

Chapter 2

Now I Lay Me Down…

WHEN I WAS in high school, I ran for class vice president four years in a row. And lost four years in a row. That was the beginning of a persistence-despite-not-getting-what-I-wanted streak for me (though, thankfully, I didn't know it at the time).

I had the same dreams that a lot of little girls had. A good marriage. A house of my own. Healthy kids when I was ready to have them, no sooner and no later. Finding a great church that would be my lifelong family. A job that would fit who I was and fill my days with productivity.

And new dreams popped up along the way…more specific dreams that matched the more specific me I was becoming. Publishing books one and two, and now three and four. Going to far-off lands. Having, for once in my life, a stretch of really great hair. Adopting internationally. Getting picked for "What Not to Wear" so I could drop $5000 of someone else's money on a new wardrobe, but being the first one to be chosen not because my wardrobe was so awful but because Stacy and Clinton were just so terribly impressed with me. Changing the world. Having my life all planned out and it being okay that I was the one who did the planning. Stuff like that.

Some of these things have panned out quite nicely, thank you very much. (Thank *You* very much.) Some, not so much at all. Some things were pleasant surprises. For instance, I wanted two daughters. Let me rephrase that. I *thought* I wanted two daughters, but I wouldn't trade my sweet Jack for anything in the world. Some things that I thought were locked in, and I hoped they would be, have up and altered themselves. My job was awesome for awhile there, now I'm a full-time stay-at-home something or other. (Which has turned out to be another immeasurably pleasant surprise, after all.)

Some of these things on my list, and others that won't make it onto these pages, have haunted me. Have completely eluded me. Sometimes after years and years of praying and hoping and watching and waiting.

My therapist, a grand woman who banters with me in metaphors and gives me lots of juicy gems to write in my journal, said to me after I shared about the day I came home to find it raining *in* my house (a long story), "Oh my…you have laid down so many things…your marriage, your job, your church, your books, your dream of adopting, and now even your home…"

Laying down. That phrase used to rub me the wrong way, sounding so passive. So…submissive. So completely admitting that you're not the one in control—and who wants to admit that?

But there's power in laying things down. Not like a New Age-y just-tell-the-universe-your-dreams-and-then-they'll-magically-come-true kind of power. No, not like that. It's the quiet power that comes with surrender. That comes with a deep breath and the even deeper admission that you not only get that you're not the one in control, but that, really, deep down, you're relieved that you're not. And this posture is in no way passive. Sometimes, it has taken every single thing in me to lay yet another thing down.

I wanted to adopt a child from Africa so desperately. From the bottom of my soul. I think of all the things I've ever wanted humanly in my life that I didn't get, this has been my biggest unrequited desire. But, as one can guess, when you're married, you really both need to be fully on board with something like this. This isn't like picking out a couch, where one can just say, "Okay, I'll learn to live with it." You don't just *learn to live with* an African child. My husband, turns out, was not on board. And not because he's a bad guy or anything; his heart is not hardened to the plight of the poor or the orphan. He prayed about it. I asked God to lead through him on this. And he returned with a no. A gentle no, but a no nonetheless. My heart ached. Deeply ached. As in, the moment he said no, I literally felt my heart hurt and had to leave the room before I started sobbing.

I could've responded in a couple ways. Absolute anger, kicking and screaming until perhaps I twisted his arm. But what kind of dream fulfillment is that? I could've moved on singing God's praises that He had a better plan and I was going to be okay. Well, that's all true and everything, but man, it hurt so much. And I wanted it *so much*. I could've held it against Kevin for the rest of our lives, but God intervened and reminded me that if I thought Kevin were able to thwart God's plan for our lives then I was giving Kevin way too much credit and God not enough.

So, this is the path I chose. I laid down my dream. I cried and cried for a little while there. And I laid it down some more. And I gave it back up to God. Sometimes I literally envisioned me placing a sweet, dark-skinned child on the altar before God, asking him to bring a Mom and Dad to the little girl who was in my head. And I would lay it down again. That wasn't all done in a few days or anything. I ached for probably a month. And I've had to lay it down again and again since then. Subconsciously, each time my close girlfriend and I would discuss her adoption process, that I was 110 percent excited about, by the way. Each time I'd read something about AIDS orphans. When I went to Haiti and visited an orphanage and each single adoptable child brushed my cheek with a gentle kiss and a whispery *bon soir* (perhaps in the hopes that this white woman would take one of them home this time). When I met my friend's daughter for the first time and watched them welcome her into their family. When I went to Africa and saw children just walking around all over the place. I have had to lay it down and lay it down and lay it down.

Turns out, each time I lay down a dream…in reality, I'm laying me down. Christ laid down His life…He had the power and choice not to. The end of our story would have been so very different had He chosen something other than what He did…had He not chosen love. And my story would be different too.

There is grace in the laying down. We find who we really are and the story plays out as was originally intended by the Author who holds all of the beginnings and endings, who knows when the plot dips and crescendos and quiets down all over again. He laid down for us, and He calls us to do the same for Him. What do you need to lay down?

Chapter 3

Joy Like a
Fountain

ON THE LAST day of my mission trip, our Africa team leader had us take out our team workbooks and write our name on the top of a blank page. We then handed the book to the person next to us to fill out something about us (I think the only directions were that it should be nice), and then we were to hand it to the next person and the next, until we had nine others' opinions of us written down in black and white. He's a really good leader. This was a really good idea. Then he had us all read our own out loud. *Whoa.* Just took it to the next level.

So, I offered to go first (I'm a "let's get things out of the way" kind of gal when it's something I don't want to do) and I must admit, I rushed through. I didn't let any of the comments really sink in, out of embarrassment, I guess. But later that evening, I pulled that list back out and one in particular struck me as so odd.

My team leader, who I knew pretty well before the trip as we had been on staff at our church together for over a year, and obviously a bit better after traveling to a third-world country and living under the same roof for ten days, had written this about me: "I appreciate your never-ending joy!"

And I thought, *Huh…did he get the right person?*

Now, I am not one of those put-myself-down-all-the-time kinds of women. I know my strengths—I'm a good leader, writer, friend, mom. I make a fabulous smoothie, I can put together a really cute outfit, I have reined in my email habit. And I know my weaknesses—I don't cook very well. I can't clean a bathtub to save my life. I drive over the speed limit, even when I'm not in a hurry (but justify it because it's usually by only 3-7 miles per hour). I am very sarcastic. I can be quite inappropriate at times. I've taken the Myers-Briggs personality test and know that I am an Introverted Intuitive Feeling Judger. I know *me*.

Most of the rest of the comments from my other teammates made me think, *Yeah, that sounds about right…that was very sweet that they said that about me…*

But joy does not come on my radar when I think about myself.

So with only this comment, I was just thinking, *Never-ending joy? That's just not who I am.*

A couple weeks after that, I was talking with a friend who said something to the effect of, "You're filled with joy and hope…" And before she could finish her sentence, I interrupted saying, "That doesn't even sound like me. I feel like I'm filled with anger and bitterness…" And she said, "But that's not the real you…the real you is joy and hope…"

Huh. Really?

So, I brought another two friends into the mix, sharing both of these incidents. One pointed to my time in Africa. She said, "Don't you remember all of your videos that you were narrating? You were practically giddy, laughing through all of them!" And the other said, "Your life may have sadness in it, but you're not responding with sadness. You're anything but bitter. That joy is the real you."

Here's the thing. Maybe joy is what God is working to bring about to completion in me. I'm telling you, these days I feel like the truest version of Beth that I've ever been. I hate the phrase "comfortable in my own skin," because usually it's being said by a twenty-something actress in the middle of her bikini photo shoot who a) doesn't have an ounce of fat on her, b) more than likely has had some kind of procedure to look the way she looks, c) hasn't been through anything truly difficult in her life, and d) is only really referring to liking what she sees when she looks in the mirror. So, I won't use that phrase. What I will say, though, is this: *I feel comfortable in my own soul.* And if I'm more *me* now than I've ever been, and people are, somehow, calling out joy as part of who that is, then maybe I can let myself go there.

Joy Like a Fountain

I have always, always, always wanted to be considered a joyful person, but have never, never, never felt like one. I absolutely love it when God uses other people to try to tell you something that He really wants you to know.

> I have loved you with an everlasting love; I have drawn you with loving-kindness. I will build you up again and you will be rebuilt, O Virgin Israel. Again you will take up your tambourines and go out to dance with the joyful.
>
> —Jeremiah 31:3 (NIV)

Chapter 4

A Freakishly Small Esophagus

THERE'S ONLY ONE reason I'm telling this story and that's because I need to be reminded, right now, that God is so enamored with us that He is still a healing God. Plus, it's a pretty cool story.

When I was a little girl, I started noticing that carrots made my mouth itch. (Hang with me—it gets better.) No biggie, I just started staying away from carrots (huge sacrifice on my part, as you can imagine). Then I started noticing that cantaloupe made my mouth itch too. Then watermelon and honeydew. Then nothing really new happened on the mouth-itching front for years.

I was in my twenties when I was in someone's apartment for the first time and within ten minutes, literally thought I had caught a cold. Full-blown. It was crazy. I realized right away that I must be having an allergic reaction to their dog. Very odd seeing as I grew up with two of my own.

Head into my thirties with me and I notice that, more and more frequently, I was finding myself choking in restaurants. Kinda weird, I know. I would cut my meat into these tiny bites and still need to run to a restroom to make myself throw it up. (I am one classy, classy lady.) It was becoming ridiculous. There wasn't a friend who hadn't experienced me holding up my index finger, as in, "wait with your story, I have to run and throw up because food is caught in my teensy little throat, but I've done this before and I'll be fine and I'll be right back…hopefully…

but maybe come check on me if I'm not back in five minutes" (yes, I can say all of that with one finger), and then they'd watch my mad dash to the restroom. I started telling people that my epitaph would read: "Elisabeth Corcoran, wife, mother, writer. Died of a freakishly small esophagus." We'd have a good laugh, but geesh, there were some pretty close calls there.

One evening I found myself at a Pampered Chef party. (I could write an entire story on the irony of that sentence alone. At least I've got the pampered part down.) As I was sitting in the back of the room with another gal, she happened to mention that she was allergic to bananas. I asked what happened to her when she ate one and she said, "They used to make my mouth itch; now my throat starts closing up." Eureka! I was *allergic* to stuff! I couldn't believe it. (How this had never even crossed my mind is a mystery to me. And pretty scary.)

Shortly after, I went to an allergist to get tested to see what foods I should avoid. If you've never done this, oh boy, are you missing out on a good time. Your back gets stuck with about thirty needles as your body responds to each potential allergen. Unless you're highly allergic. Which, apparently, I was. They had to stop halfway through and give me epinephrine because my back was covered with red, itchy spots and they didn't think my body could handle any more in one sitting.

So I had to go back a week later to finish the testing. When done, the doctor and I had a little chat. She looked at my list of allergens and sighed. I said, jokingly, "Maybe it would be easier for you to start with the foods I actually *can* eat." I grinned, thinking surely she'd never heard that one before. "You're probably right," she said. (*Gulp*, I thought.) "Water…" Pause. I'm not kidding. She actually said "water" and then had to pause. "Rice…" Pause. "Oats…" Pause. I finally just interrupted and said, "Water, rice and oats? Ummm…maybe can you just go back to telling me what I can't eat? Because right now, you're completely freaking me out."

My allergist went on to list about thirty-five or forty food items I needed to stay away from, or at least be cautious of. And she prescribed an epi-pen and showed me how to use it on myself (that's the thing you're supposed to shove into your own thigh in case of an allergy emergency). Oh, and I was also officially allergic to cats, dogs, dust, pollen, grass, and trees. So the world, basically. I was allergic to creation. Interesting. I should stay away from outside, inside, and food. But I could have water, rice, and oats, so all was not lost. The parties I could throw with water, rice, and oats...

Fast forward a year or so and I found myself at my favorite retreat center. They make yummy meals for you that make you feel very taken care of. Meal time is one of my favorite times on retreat. But one of these times, I bellied up to the little buffet and realized, sadly, that the only thing I could safely eat that had been prepared for me was a piece of white bread with a side of water. How pathetic. So I'm sitting there eating my bread, trying to make it last, just looking out the window at the beautiful scenery and for some reason my mind drifts to thinking it reminds me of what Eden might've looked like. And then my thought goes on one step further, and I think to myself, "This isn't what God intended for me. Food is a gift. He wants me to be able to eat all foods." And I did something that had never, ever occurred to me to do, I'm ashamed to admit. I prayed. Right then and there, after twenty plus years of food allergies, I asked God to heal me. That's all I said. And I'll be honest, I didn't give it a whole lot of thought after that.

Right before that retreat, I had looked into getting allergy shots. Not that they can cure you of food allergies, but apparently if you're taking these shots, they can lessen your other allergies, which in turn lessen the severity of any food allergy reactions you may have. I was tired of running to restrooms in public, so I was kicking this around. Only problem—it would cost $10,000 and wasn't covered on my husband's insurance. That was a fairly significant problem.

(Here's an aside, but it's a funny aside. I was meeting with my allergist to discuss the whole shot thing and he asks me how old I am. I say thirty-two and he says, "I would have guessed twenty-six..." (*Why thank you, sir*, I'm thinking...except he wasn't finished talking...) "... except for your age-inappropriate dark under-eye circles. While you're here, you can go have those looked at...I know a good plastic surgeon in the building." *Umm, I pretty much just want to talk about getting my allergy shots and not how desperately I'd benefit from getting some work done, but thanks.*)

So I'm sharing this entire story with my Dad and he actually gave me a check for $10,000 so I could get the shots. It was an incredibly generous gift. I was beside myself. I decided to head back to the allergist to get re-tested for my allergies so that if I were really going to do this shot thing and dump $10,000 of my father's money into it, I'd make sure I was getting the exact concoction for my specific allergy mix.

I'm in the allergist's office, maybe a month or two after my retreat, and therefore after my retreat prayer, getting all of the same tests done about a year after my original allergy testing. I'm noticing that I'm not feeling any itching as the tests are being done, and I start praying feverishly. *Heal me from these, Jesus! I know You can. This would be a miracle!*

The doctor comes in to share with me the results. She starts the list. These are the things I was allergic to that day: green peas…walnuts. That was it! Jesus had healed me of my allergies. My mouth hasn't itched in years. I can eat all of my original listed no-no's with abandon. I praise God when I bite into cantaloupe or dip a carrot into ranch dressing.

I'm not allergic to the world anymore. And do you know why? Because our loving God is still a healing God.

A Little Divine and Wife Intervention, Please

THIS IS THE story of how my husband landed his current job, thanks to me. Funny how even when I'm telling someone else's story, I somehow find myself in a leading role. Well, a) that's human nature, b) I *am* the one telling it, and c) it's actually true in this case. I got him his job. Although it's interesting that he always balks at that little fact. I'll let you be the judge.

We had been married for six months. I was "finding myself" (i.e. unemployed except for the very occasional temp job) and Kevin was on his first year of teaching at a small Christian school. I hate to say this, but all these years later we still refer to it as the "year from hell." It was a very difficult employment situation for him. Add to that, we lived *in* the school. I won't even begin to paint that picture for you, but I will say this much—our bedroom door was fifteen steps from his junior high classroom. Need I say more? Oh, and one more little fairly key piece of information. He made $10,600. Let me point out that this was 1994. Not *1964*. Our take-home was $600 a month. Our rent (for living *in the school*) was $300. Do the math. Times were tight. I had a $25-a-week grocery budget and we went out to dinner once a month at Chi-Chi's. Oh, the good ol' days. (I hated the good ol' days.) But God kindly sustained us despite living below the poverty line.

The year was winding down. We had sent out countless resumes. We both desperately wanted out of that horrible situation. Kevin had been given a contract for the following school year. We were praying with everything in us to not have to sign it, but the deadline of Friday, May 27 was looming before us. We didn't want to be irresponsible so we agreed that we would sign it if he didn't have an offer from another school by that date. Man, oh man, did we pray.

One morning in mid-May, I was planning on attending a women's spring brunch at our new church. I didn't want to go. I was and am a flaming introvert. I hated things like that. (Funny how God would end up steering me in the direction to become our church's first ever official Women's Ministry Director and have me end up planning innumerable events just like that one.) But I told myself to go because after six months, I really needed to start meeting people. It was tough going to a church of mostly young families when you're newlyweds and kid-less…we just didn't feel like we fit in yet. But I felt like I was "supposed" to go. Like it was a God thing. So I put it on my calendar and went on with my life.

The night before the event, I chose my outfit and set my alarm, all nauseous because I didn't want to go. The next morning dawned and Kevin was already up and gone on an all-day hunting trip with a friend. I looked at that alarm and thought to myself, *Kevin's not here to hold me accountable. No one will know if I don't show up.* I turned off my alarm and went back to sleep.

I don't tend to have very clear dreams, but I had one in those moments. I dreamt that I woke up too late to attend the event and I was furious with myself for missing it. I woke up immediately knowing that was a nudge from God but certain it now really was too late to go since I'd gone back to sleep. Turns out, I had only slept for seven more minutes. I had plenty of time.

I got ready, more nervous than before because now God was involved, and headed to church. I could not tell you what we ate or what the speaker talked about. In fact, I started heading out of the auditorium thinking, *What was the big deal? Why did You want me here so badly?*

On my way out, I ran into a gal named Martha, who had been very friendly to me those past few months. She had been a home economics teacher and asked how Kevin's school year was going. I told her it wasn't all that great and we were desperately praying for another job to open up, but nothing had. And we figured by now that nothing would, as most positions were filled for the start of the coming school year by early spring. I also told her that we were on a deadline to sign the other contract and how much we both didn't want to.

She mentioned fairly casually that her former principal was a Christian, in a really good public school district, and that if I brought Kevin's resume with me to church the next day, she'd drop it off on Monday with a personal recommendation, which she ended up doing for us. Kevin received a phone call from that principal on Tuesday, had an interview on Wednesday, and received a job offer (for three times his current salary, mind you) on Thursday, May 26. Remember when I said the deadline was to sign the contract with the school we didn't want to stay at? Yep, Friday the 27th.

And none of it would've happened had I skipped that event. In other words, I got him his job. It was all because of me. Oh yeah, and our incredibly providing God.

Chapter 6

He'll Redeem Anything

THIS IS THE story of how I started the Women's Ministry at my sweet little church, what used to be called Blackberry Creek Community. It's not a grand story. In fact, it paints me in a rather horrible light. But sometimes the best lessons can come from other people messing up and being jerks.

I had struggled with the demise of a friendship. A friendship that had meant quite a lot to me. It was basically my first, real "grown-up" friendship after getting married and starting to attend our church. I thought I found someone that I really clicked with. And I had. And we ended up spending a great deal of time together. But I screwed up. And then I went on to add insult to injury in the sloppy way I tried to fix it. So we parted ways. Not officially, but we just slowly stopped seeing each other, and not chatting for a long time at church anymore and such. It was heartbreaking for me, because I really loved this gal.

Fast forward a bit…I had given birth to my daughter, Sara, and was looking for ways to get out of the house, just a bit. I even said yes to things like Longaberger Basket parties. I know. So, one day, while at one of these kinds of parties, where I had no intention of buying anything and only the intention of not being in charge of diapers for a while, a mutual friend and my old friend walked in. I immediately felt butterflies, as in, *how awkward is this going to be?* Let me tell ya, it was awkward.

She had a little boy about six months older than Sara, and at the end of that party, while we were getting coats on and such, my old friend and the mutual friend began talking about starting a play group for their two kids. Mind you, I'm about six inches away from them. (At least in my head, I was standing that close.) And they began tossing names around of who else they could invite. Now, as most moms know, a play group with infants, babies, and toddlers is about ten times more for the sanity of the mothers than it is for the development of the children. In my head I'm screaming, "Invite *me*! Ask *me*! Am I invisible? I'm lonely! I'm trying to figure out this mom thing and I am just sure I'm doing it all wrong! *I want to be in your play group!*" But they continued to list off a few other gals, completely ignoring me. My heart was shattered. It brought up all of my childhood friend issues. I cried all the way home.

But then, I dug in my heels. I took that feeling…that feeling of being ignored and unwelcomed…and told myself that no woman should feel that way, especially in Christian circles. So I called up our interim pastor at church and asked if I could start some kind of mom's group or women's something or other. Anything, really. He referred me to another gal at church who had also just that week contacted him with the same idea (there are no coincidences in the Kingdom of God, ladies and gentlemen) and told me to get ahold of her.

I met with that sweet woman the following week and we began what would end up being a beautiful friendship and a ten-year reign for us as co-Women's Ministry Directors at our church. A small handful of women came to Christ over those ten years. I'm hoping many were encouraged in their faith, their marriages, and their mothering along the way. Many figured out their spiritual gifts through serving, and what their gifts were not, which is equally important in my mind. I gave one of my first talks during that time and learned I had the gifts of leadership and teaching all through that. And it all started with spite. That's the ugly part I was talking about.

But here's the takeaway…God doesn't just redeem us from our sin. He can redeem our choices and our past and our impure motives and our selfish ambitions, and He can turn them around and use them for His genuine good. I didn't want other women to be hurt like I was hurt… thankfully, lovingly, God had a whole other thing in mind.

Chapter 7

Deep Calls to Deep

IHAVE A FRIEND who is one of the coolest people I've ever met. Like, I wonder why, really, she likes to hang out with me when I'm old (in comparison) and not nearly as cool. But we get along really well, we can talk about pretty much anything, and we've seen each other through none-too-few crises. Like, really, in the past seven or so years since we've been friends, one or both of us have been in deep weeds in some way, shape, or form at any given time. But we've walked the various roads together…waiting in hospitals, waiting on freeways, waiting in church sanctuaries, waiting in an airport for a little girl to arrive from Africa, waiting in a courtroom for a verdict, little things like that. (Don't get me wrong…it's not like we just sit around playing the Death March, while wearing black and writing poetry about our collective sorrows… we *do* actually have fun together…)

So the other day, she and I were on a walk, and I asked what was new. She said something like, "Ummm, almost nothing. Things are…good… *normal,*" she said almost hesitantly as if a bolt of lightning would strike us both dead on the spot for daring to admit that. And we kind of looked at each other and I think I said, "Wow, what's that like?" and then we laughed. We almost didn't know how to do just small talk. Not when we've together tackled the issues of life that we've covered over the years.

Which got me thinking. And maybe this is just me. But I'm finally beginning to see that life is just one hard thing after another with, hopefully, some breaks in between to refuel. I think I've had in the back of my head that surely one day the hard stuff would stop and I would have a really long remission. But I don't think it's like that. Granted, I know some people who somehow skate through life. Who really have had almost nothing hugely bad happen to them. I don't know if I really get those people. Because there is such a depth to people who've really been hammered by life but keep getting up again. I love people like that.

Not that there's anything wrong with having nothing bad happen to you…I'm not saying you should go out and drum up some tragedies or something just to muster a bit of character development, but I think there is a huge difference in a person who's been through a thing or two compared to a person who hasn't.

And this may sound odd, but I actually love plumbing the depths of a hard situation. Maybe that's the melancholy part of me talking. But there's almost a part of me that says *bring it on*. I should probably keep that to myself.

What are you going through these days? Is it a heavy burden that's dragging you down? Walk through it with a friend, and walk through it with God, letting Him hold your hand and carry you through…just keep walking.

He wants to bring you healing. The question is, "Do you want to be made well?"

Chapter 8

So I Sinned, Now What?

NOW ON TO one of my sin stories. Who doesn't love a good sin story, right? But before I just jump right in, I want to talk about how I perceive sin. I believe that because God is holy all sin is equal in His eyes. Equally wrong and equally repulsive. Even though our minds see things like murder and a white lie as different, I believe God sees all sin the same. However, with all that said, I humanly see two kinds of sin. There's the yelling at our kids, sinning in our anger, kind of sin. The kind of thing where you didn't mean to do it, it's something you are trying to work on, you hate when you do it, you feel terrible about, and hopefully you try to repair right away most of the time. Then there's this other kind. This is the kind that I want to share with you.

Several years ago, I got myself into a sinful situation. I have debated whether or not to share the exact sin because mainly I don't want you to look at mine and hold it up to something in your life and think, "oh, my thing isn't that bad..." or whatever, and then not feel you need to deal with it. But on the other hand, I was afraid that if I didn't outright say what it was, wandering imaginations may do more damage than the truth. Besides, I believe with everything in me that when God looks at my heart, He sees Christ, and not my past sin. As Colossians 1:22 (NIV) says, "But now He has reconciled you by Christ's physical body through death to present you holy in His sight, without blemish and free from accusation." So I'm about to lay myself out here...and I'm trusting that God will soften your hearts toward me in this process, but if He doesn't, that's not up to me.

Basically, here's what happened. Long story short, after years of arguments over money, my husband and I decided that I should get a monthly allowance. We agreed upon an amount that would cover all my regular expenses like if I wanted to go out for dinner with a girlfriend down to clothes and shoes for the kids and for me. It worked great for a while until I noticed that I was spending all my money before I would get my allowance. Meaning, I was charging everything, and then as soon as I would get my allowance, I would send that into Citibank and be broke for another month, but I'd just use my credit card again in the meantime. I was fine as long as I paid off my monthly balance, which I was doing for a while there; but then I got in over my head. I was too ashamed to talk to Kevin about it, so I just tried to take care of it on my own. But it was plaguing me—my money troubles were all I thought about. Until one day, my generous father sent us a check in the mail, made out to me, but it was actually for us as a couple to put toward our church building campaign. Well, in the moments after seeing that check, this is what crossed my mind, "This is your chance to get caught up! No one has to know!" And so without batting an eye, I deposited half of it in my checking account and the other half in our joint account, and then led Kevin to believe we had only received half of the actual amount from my Dad.

My money troubles were momentarily over, but here's what happened…I became depressed. I lost all physical energy. All spiritual desire for closeness with God, for ministry…gone. I was even *less* patient with my kids and Kevin. And I was considering getting a prescription for anti-depressants. I was a mess. As Beth Moore calls it, I was *sin sick*, without a doubt…though I was basically in denial about the cause.

Several months went by of my holding in my secret, but then something happened. I decided at the last minute to go away with a group of girls to a Women of Faith conference. Before I went, I wrote Kevin a letter of confession and apology (I'm such a wuss—*a letter*—I even hid it under his pillow, partly hoping he wouldn't find it!). And I went knowing that confessing to just Kevin was not enough. I knew I had to tell someone outside of just him and me. James 5:16 (MSG) says: "Make this your common practice: confess your sins to each other and pray for each other so that you live together whole and healed." That previous year, I had been in an accountability relationship with two other women from church, who both happened to be going to the conference. In between one of the sessions, I confessed everything…all the awful, sinful details, crying my way through it. And then something divine happened. I looked up and realized they were crying with me. And then they prayed for me. They didn't show judgment, just grace and love. Second Corinthians 2:7 (MSG) says: "Now is the time to forgive this man and help him back on his feet. If all you do is pour on the guilt, you could very well drown him in it." And that is exactly what those two precious friends did for me…they were God's forgiveness to me. I felt such peace – for the first time in several months. Because I no longer had a secret. I couldn't be found out – because I had already narced on myself. And then one of them said, "What can we do to help you?" My initial response was asking them to ask me how I'm doing with my spending from time to time. But then she said, "Why don't you cut up your credit card?" I immediately panicked thinking I could never live without one…but within an hour or so, I had broken it in two and handed them the pieces.

I went home, feeling lighter and more peaceful than I'd been in months, but I knew I still had my husband to face. I came home and he gave me the sweetest hug. To which I replied, "You must not have found my letter!" He said he did and that we could talk after the kids went to bed. That in itself was him showing me grace. And he showed me even more…I begged him for forgiveness, and he gave it to me. He held me while I cried and I just let months of self-anger and sadness out.

During my depression, I had journaled about all of the areas that were possibly affected by my four months of intentionally covering up my sin. And it hit me one day that I won't know until heaven. It doesn't say there are no tears in heaven, it says that Jesus will wipe all our tears away. That season of my life will no doubt bring me to tears as I see all the damage that I did in that time. All the blessings and prayers I blocked. All the kingdom work that could have been done.

But I live in the peace that God is bigger than my sin and that He has every intention of continuing to restore me, and to move even through that time in my life. Oswald Chambers said, "Then that very (sin) itself, and all that you have been through in connection with it, will glorify Jesus Christ in a way that you will never know until you see Him to face to face." So I will one day see the good that came from that situation.

And in fact, I already have. I went on to make restitution, paying every cent back. I told my pastor, and I wrote a talk about it and confessed to the women of my church. I made amends to my Dad who, amazingly, graciously said, "Baby, if you're looking for forgiveness, you've got it." And I even told my children about it, teaching them the process of messing up, fixing it, asking for forgiveness, then receiving it, and moving on.

I messed up. But the grace I have felt since has compelled me to live as authentically as I know how…wanting people to love me for who I really am, wanting to love people for who they really are.

Chapter 9

Time at the Shore

I AM CURRENTLY ON the receiving end of a tremendously generous gift. A friend knew I was in need of some "let's get outta here" time and she proposed the kind of idea that can only fly after twenty-two years of friendship. That we go away together, spend our days on our own, and meet up each evening for dinner. Oh, and she has a friend who will let us use her on-the-beach cabin in Michigan. I couldn't type the words "I'm so in" fast enough. And that brings us to this moment.

I am propped up in bed, looking out a huge window at Lake Michigan, scratching some mosquito bites from last night's talk-on-the-beach-watching-the-sun-go-down-and-the-stars-come-out session, while sipping a glass of wine and writing a little something.

I've never had a glass of wine by myself before. In fact, before last night under the stars, I'd never had a glass of wine, period. What am I, thirteen? Apparently, according to my friend, it's not even all that good. I wouldn't know. Wine is wine to me. I think it makes me feel like a grown-up. A real writer. I picture real grown-up writers sitting leisurely at their desks in their studies in their mansions, sipping wine and cranking out their next best seller. And I think I'm also drinking it because, who knows, maybe I'm funnier with a little wine in me. Which I doubt, because a) I'm pretty funny to begin with, and b) it's not a magic potion…and it probably takes a good half hour to kick in. Anyway, where was I?

Oh yes, the beach. I've noticed that I place certain experiences upon a pedestal. Beach excursions fall into this category. They are so much better in my head than in reality. Like, in my head, the water isn't cold, the air temperature isn't too hot or too chilly, the bugs don't bite, and the chairs aren't uncomfortable. But it is and they do and they are. Don't get me wrong. It has been wonderful. My biggest responsibility has been to remember to eat every few hours. I could do this all summer. So know that I am not complaining. But I was sitting down there on the shore, and I was simultaneously wiping my forehead with my hand because it was about five degrees warmer than my body likes, swatting at biting flies, and picking off me little bits of what I can only describe as cotton-ball size wads of pollen flying all around me like snow. I finally just stood up and said, "Forget it. It's not worth it."

But other than that slightly frustrating encounter, it has been pure delight. I've started each morning—and when I say each, I mean the past two out of two—with a run on the beach (harder than they make it look on television…now I know why the opening sequence of Baywatch was in slow motion), a smoothie and a shower, a quiet time and a cup of tea on the beach, a few minutes of feet-digging-into-the-wet-sand yoga, and then pretty much hours of cycling in and out of sitting/thinking/journaling/reading and going up to the house for something to snack on, then back to the beach to sit/think/journal/read some more. Night finds us meeting up at about five to go out to eat (not because we're senior citizens but because we're still on Chicago time), and back to the house for a movie and maybe some star-gazing.

We head back home tomorrow already. It feels like we've been here about five minutes. Like I said, I really could do this all summer. I needed to get away. Needed to do nothing. Needed to not feel guilty doing nothing or be watched by my husband and kids doing nothing. Needed to not be in my usual environment, doing my usual tasks, in my usual circumstances. Needed to be away enough to think about where things stand in my relationships and in my soul. Gifts like this—of time away just when needed—are so intimate, feel so loving…I've felt tended to here…looked after. I've already gotten much soul work done…but again, I could do this all summer. I think the wine helps.

II

Once upon a time, there was a girl who...

...met some people and was loved by God...

Chapter 10

Oh, My Sweet Girls

WHEN I WAS young, I had this knack of befriending a little girl who happened to have an already-established best friend waiting in the wings. We'd hang out for a while and inevitably she'd go back to her old best friend. Now, this did not happen to me just once or twice. Let me tell you how many times this happened to me... Jessica chose Catherine over me, Jennifer chose Chris over me, Barb chose Michelle over me, Joely chose Donina over me, Michelle chose Lisa over me, Lori chose Jenna over me...it was nuts. And it was sad. My heart was constantly re-breaking over the repeated rejection...I just wanted a friend to call my own!

Gratefully, God stepped in. In one month's time, I was introduced to my first real best friend (sweet Keely) and my eternal best friend, Jesus. That was a grand month. He brought healing to me through those two relationships and started to renovate my view of friendship. He brought me out of the place of being a girl-hater, thinking all were posers and/or catty, and brought me into a new place, where I ended up, ironically, leading the Women's Ministry at my church (whoever thinks God doesn't have a fantastic sense of humor just doesn't know how to look at it) and into a place of an abundance of kind, thoughtful, godly, hysterical, creative, brave, beautiful women to call my friends.

But every once in a while I still need to remind myself of the importance of good friends. This is going to be one of those times. I just got back from a long weekend out of town with three girlfriends (thanks to my Dad's outrageous generosity). We had an absolute blast—great food, spa treatments, poolside cabana fruity drinks, fantastic shows… it was a terrific time. But add to that, leisurely conversations that could be as silly or as deep as we wanted because we had all the time in the world, and you get a combination of hysterical laughter and many tear-filled moments. It was beautiful. Those four days are etched in my memory way more, not because of the limo rides and mani/pedis, but because it was four days of sweet memory-building with women who mean the world to me.

And it leaves me wondering if I'm in the minority. As a little girl, I struggled for years and years to find even one trustworthy friend. Then my twenties found me with an abundance of female relationships but most of them were not the depth my heart was searching for. And now I find myself in my thirties with several years of the same close girlfriends that I can trust my heart and life with. And I do everything I can to not take them for granted, or even the fact that I have them. I have been so blessed in this area. But I wonder if having "my girls" is unusual. If most women my age might not. I hope that's not the case. I hope my experience with my friends is what most women who love God have in their lives, because they are expressions of Christ's love to me, and I hope I am to them from time to time too.

I couldn't have gotten through a certain crisis a while back without them and I wouldn't want to celebrate life's highpoints without them either. They hold my hand, cry with me, laugh with me, pray for me, write me notes, make me meals, leave me great voicemails, send me encouraging emails, give me fabulous compliments, talk kindly to me and about me, will be taking my secrets to their graves, know me pretty darn well, and still, somehow, think I'm great. As do I with each of them.

Do you have this in your life? I hope you do. I believe God designed us to be in relationship—with our husbands if we're married, yes; but also with other women who understand us in a way men just can't (at no fault of their own). If our husbands would have seen how often we teared up this past weekend, they would have thought we were insane…but we knew better, and just instinctively passed around the Kleenex™.

If you're looking for a good friend, I have a few ideas for you. Ask God for one…He already knows what and who you need. Let Him pursue you through authentic and fun relationships with other women. Begin to be the kind of friend you want—go the extra mile, be trustworthy to a fault—to someone already in your life. Initiate a conversation or a date for coffee…someone has to go first and it might as well be you. Choose well and wisely—not everyone needs to know every single thing about your life and heart. But do risk, do let someone in, do let someone take care of you every once in awhile. And once you've got her, thank God for her and pour out your life into her. You'll be so glad you did.

Chapter 11

Welcome Home, Little Girl

THREE HOURS AGO at O'Hare International Airport, I met a precious little three-year-old girl (who is even more beautiful than her pictures prepared us for) for the first time—and watched her mommy, sister, brother, and grandmothers meet her too. (Her daddy and grampa had gone to Africa to get her and bring her home.) Two of my dearest friends just fulfilled a dream of theirs—they adopted a little girl from Ethiopia.

I cried like a baby. I've got this running list of "top ten best moments in my life." Among them are the births of my kids. Baptizing my mom is on that list. Going to Haiti is on that list. Experiencing Africa firsthand is on that list. And meeting Selamawit is now on that list. There are some moments in time when words, no matter how good the words, just cannot paint an accurate picture. Because something magical, mystical, otherworldly, bigger than us was taking place in those moments, when a new and somehow better version of an already amazing family came to be.

I had two thoughts. Okay, I've had about a hundred thoughts, but I'm going to share two. The first thought was that what I was watching happen was light breaking through the darkness. Selamawit's Ethiopian future was grim. Pretty much anyone's is unfortunately, but a little girl in poverty in Ethiopia doesn't really stand a chance. What they did in intervening to bring this little girl home to a real childhood is nothing short of glorious and miraculous. And they had an enemy that didn't want this light to break through…but they fought against it and Light won out. Love won out. It usually does, by the way, in case you find yourself currently wondering.

And the second thing…I watched her daddy hoist her up onto his shoulders from very far away and saw her mommy, my sweet friend, go running to meet them…and then I saw her whisper, "I love you." My friend already loves her daughter. Her daughter that she hadn't met until that moment. Her daughter who, technically, hadn't done anything to earn her love. She loves her…*deeply*. And I thought how this story sounded so familiar to me. Romans 5:8 (MSG) says, "God put His love on the line for us by offering His Son in sacrificial death while we were of no use to Him whatsoever." Selamawit had nothing to offer my friend and her family…we have nothing at all to offer God. Yet He woos us. He calls us by name. He considers us precious and honored. He pays a high price for us. He loves us in a way we'll never understand…and has before we paid Him any attention. And He takes it one step further…He offers us the opportunity to become a part of His family. Listen to Ephesians 1:5 (MSG): "Long, long ago, He decided to adopt us into His family through Jesus Christ. (What pleasure He took in planning this!)" Selamawit, before even being picked up in Ethiopia, had become a legal part of this family. And though it was a hard year with all the paperwork and waiting, what pleasure they took in planning for her.

A family was re-created today. And it was magnificent. One of the most beautiful things I've ever seen. And God extends His hand of family and friendship to you and to me. If you've accepted Christ as your Savior, you're already a part of the family. But if you haven't, you can. The offer stands. You may not know God yet, but He knows you. He studies your face the way my friend and her husband studied Selamawit's pictures on their fridge. He knows your name…He calls you by name…just like they practiced her name with their last name time and again. He wants to be your Abba Father…which means, basically, *Daddy*. And who of us wouldn't benefit from the healing that comes from an intimate relationship with the One who created us and has loved us since before time began? I know the day that I called on His name for the first time is number one on my top ten life moments list. And it can be the same for you.

By the way, that sweet little girl came off the plane from Africa wearing a Gap Inspi(red)™ T-shirt...she inspired me, that's for sure. How I can't wait to run into my loving Abba Father's arms when all of this is said and done.

Chapter 12

A Well Loved Woman

I AM A CHRISTIAN woman married to a Christian man and our marriage has been, and is, difficult. I am, at times, a lonely married woman. My husband is not only aware of this, he is in the same boat as I am. And as much as I know how shocking those statements can look in black and white, I know that I know that I know that I am not the only woman out there who feels this way.

Before I go on, let me tell you why I'm writing about this. Because I've had too many women walk up to me after a speaking engagement and bend down, with tears in their eyes, and whisper a confession that they are in a hard marriage. I can tell that, for the most part, I am the first person they are telling this to. And my heart breaks for each and every one of them. Because I know what they are feeling and because it kills me that they each think they're the only ones who are going through this, and that they feel the need to keep it to themselves. So I'm writing this as liberation. First, for me: to take off the mask so that each of my readers knows that no, I do not have my act all together. And for you…you, the reader, so that you can know for a fact that no, you are *not* alone, sweet girl.

For reasons that I am not going to go into here, my marriage is hard. Like, harder than the average hard. (And my husband would agree.) Over the years, I have struggled with every emotion over this fact—from denying its reality, to anger with God for letting this happen, to anger with myself for the choices I made that got me to where we are today, to resignation, to loss of hope, to now…utter determination.

Because somewhere along the way, I started to realize something. I am a much, much stronger woman and follower of Jesus because of my difficult marriage. That's right—I said *because*.

And I have noticed something shifting in me over the years. Subtle changes in how I have come to respond to the marriage disappointments. Softer words. Less anger. Less bitterness. Fewer tears along the way... though I know I've cried a river in my lifetime, fewer tears come these days. A defiant, stubborn bravery has replaced my resignation.

That really, if a demanding marriage is the biggest obstacle I have to deal with for the rest of my life...if that is what God is calling me to...I can do that for another fifty years. I don't have HIV, my kids don't bathe in dirty puddles of water that they also must drink from, I'm healthy and have my wits about me, I've got friends and I've got Jesus. So if this is my thorn in the flesh then God's grace is more than enough for me. And what He's showing me is that He is, indeed, completely enough for me, through and through.

I know that some of you may have already walked away from marriage circumstances not as difficult as mine. And some of you will stay through things I can't even imagine. And there is grace enough to cover it all. There is grace and grace and more grace for each one of you...for each one of us.

But for those of us who are staying, let me say this. There is a beauty in the holding on when you don't think you can anymore. And, frankly, as this isn't all that practical in our day-to-day lives, I'm not sure if this will come as encouragement to you or not...but it does to me when I let it sink in. There is a beauty in the hoping that there will be a few more jewels in my marriage crown *just because I stayed* that will help me honor Christ more when I see Him face to face.

But here's some good news. I'm growing. I'm being restored. I'm being healed. *We're* being healed. God does still heal, if you're wondering. Our circumstances are changing for the deep better, I can say gratefully. And even though a circumstance may stay relatively the same for the rest of your life, you, my friend, can change and grow and be renewed inwardly day by day by day.

I heard a woman I admire from afar say that she is a "well-loved woman" in reference to her husband. I heard that and cringed. I am happy for her. In that kind of I-wish-I-were-her-for-fifteen-minutes way. I don't always feel like a well-loved woman. I'm sure my husband would say he doesn't always feel like a well-loved man, either. I cannot stress enough that this is not a woe-is-me scenario or a one-way relational street I'm walking down. I think, actually, that we can all say that. Human beings let other human beings down. A lot.

But recently, I've stumbled upon a song that has deeply nourished my soul.

"I Receive Your Love for Me"

I receive Your everlasting love for me
I receive Your everlasting love for me

Nothing I can say
Will take Your love away
No place I can go
Where Your love won't be there
Nothing I can do
Will make You love me more
Your love comes as a gift
And I only have to open it

I receive Your everlasting love for me
I receive Your everlasting love for me

I receive Your love for me
I receive Your love for me

©1994 Mercy / Vineyard Publishing

And in the moment when I first heard that song, I brought up the words of that fortunate wife, and I thought to myself, *Ah yes…I can say that about myself after all.* I can't do anything to generate more love from God because He is already loving me to the full. Loving me more than my mind and heart can even comprehend, which means only one thing. I *am* a well-loved woman.

And dear friend, so are you.

Chapter 13

Nothing Like I Thought

I WAS AMBUSHED LAST night. Blind-sided. A bait-and-switch took place with my heart. I actually think God might be smiling down on me just a bit because He knows that just the fact that I'm writing about it, let alone so soon, shows that I've let the healing start to break in, even if in small pieces, and that's a good sign.

A person who sometimes falls under the category of "my nemesis," whom I'll call Chris, and I went to dinner with someone else, whom I'll call Alex, as part of a Matthew 18 thing. You know, the passage about going to a third party to work something out. I went, to be truthful, to watch Chris get a tongue-lashing, at least a little bit. That was even me being all prayed up. Kind of scary, I know.

Surprise, surprise. Didn't happen. I went thinking Alex would look Chris in the eye and tell Chris to stop doing what he was doing (i.e. hurting me). Alex sort of did that. With about as much condemnation as grounding yourself for getting a B on an exam, which I've done, so I know it's not all that convicting, nor does it force any kind of lasting change.

But then Alex brought up about ten things in me that he somehow made out to sound even worse than what Chris was doing to me. Like I said, blind-sided. Kicked in the gut. I never saw it coming.

Oh, it gets better. Alex actually implied that part of why Chris does what Chris does might just be because of, basically, who I am as a person. I could possibly be driving Chris to this pattern of hurting me. Something to look into, at least, Alex said. Tears stung in my eyes and ran down my face and I had to excuse myself from the table.

What about Chris? He's the one doing all the hurting! I was screaming in my head as I stood in the bathroom.

But here is just the tip of the healing. (Trust me—this one's going to take a while.) Remember how I mentioned I was prayed up? I really had been. I had asked God to speak through Alex to both of us. (I forgot to ask for the strength to bear up under the weight of what He might want to say to little ol' me, I guess…) But though each word was hard to hear, and though I'd still give anything for someone to smack Chris in the head on my behalf (in a Christian way, of course…like maybe with a Bible or an offering plate), I can't escape the fact that God is big enough for this.

God knew that those words were on their way to my heart and how much they were going to devastate me, let alone in the middle of my current state—brokenhearted and numb. But He let them be said to me anyway. Now, I can't dismiss that Alex is human and maybe spoke out of turn in some instances, maybe not fully understanding the scope of our complicated situation. Or that my real enemy (the enemy of my soul) is pretty darn pleased with how that evening shook out, me crying in my van all the way home and into the shower, completely wondering if I am so horrible of a person that, of course, I drove Chris to hurt me over and over again. To wonder why more people don't go out of their way to hurt me if I'm all this rotten.

But after walking around really sad…like defeated sad…all day today, I took a nap, did some reading, and remembered that so much more is going on in my life than what I can see with my own two eyes. And then, better late than never, I asked God to help me see what He wants me to see in last night's conversation…but even more so, for the strength and grace to handle what He's got for me in all of it…even if I don't like at all what I hear. And even in this surprise pain, I know God is chasing me down with His love. Because He loves me enough to let the hard words come, to help me move farther along on the journey.

Chapter 14

And Then There's Grace

I HAD A BAD night two nights ago (see previous essay). But I had a good, good morning this morning. I went to yoga, per usual on Monday mornings, then stopped over at the house of the mother of a dear friend. This woman has become like a second mom to me. She is so dear. We have weathered many a health crisis of her daughter's and of her grandson's together. Anyway, she's one of the most godly women I know. And here's how I describe godly: she deeply knows and loves Jesus, and you can tell she knows that He deeply knows and loves her too. You just feel like you're with Jesus when you're with this lady. Her life has not always been an easy one, and since I am going through a little something, I thought she might be able to offer me some wisdom, maybe pray for me. She made me a cup of tea, served some apple slices (she's just so sweet, I wish you could all know her), listened attentively, and shared parts of her journey with me.

Her gentleness healed so much of the wounds that I felt I received two nights ago. She will call sin, sin, but what she called out over me was grace. She actually told me to stop trying so hard. (Funny, that's the opposite of what Alex and Chris want to see me do...they think I'm not working nearly hard enough on this relationship.) She told me to "cease striving." As in "Cease striving and know that I am God," (Psalm 46:10 NASB). She told me to abide in the deep love that Christ has for me. She told me to focus on being kind, and nothing else. Then she held my hands and prayed for me and my situation.

She was Christ to me in those two hours. God loved me so much to send healing through this precious woman. She said words that my soul so desperately needed to hear. I drove home with the window rolled down, on a not fully spring morning, but just because it felt like the right thing to do at the time. I drove under the speed limit along windy back roads. I sang along softly with Sara Groves. And then I walked through my front door with new, simpler, doable, gentler marching orders.

Cease. Abide. Show kindness. I can do that. Christ in me *can* do that. Oh, thank You, Jesus. Sigh…

Chapter 15

Guard Your Heart

I HAD BEEN MEETING with a friend a few years younger than me in a sort of informal discipling relationship. She'd come over to my house while my kids napped and we'd go through a book together. I think we did this for about a year and I really enjoyed her company.

One day I was sharing something with her about my marriage that was pretty personal. I was sharing it in an I-know-how-you-feel kind of way after she'd shared something with me. I didn't think twice about sharing this thing with her because we'd known each other quite a while and I trusted her.

I just didn't know that she and I differed on one small, yet fairly pivotal, life truth. That being my belief that "what is said in the room stays in the room." I thought this was held worldwide. I was wrong.

She came back a couple weeks later, and fairly casually said, "Yeah, I told my husband about that thing with you and Kevin..." I sort of drowned out every word beyond that. I'm surprised I didn't fall off the couch right then and there. I can't remember if I said this or was just screaming this in my head, but here's what I was thinking. "If your husband had been sitting there on the couch with you that day, I never in a million years would have shared what I shared about Kevin and me." I must've said something to that effect, because I remember her saying something like, "Well, he and I are one, so he can know what I know…" *Wow, that would've been nice to know two weeks ago*, I growled to myself.

I was blown away. I felt betrayed, and yet, more than anything, upset with myself for divulging more than I should have. I had a mess to clean up. I had to tell Kevin that two people knew about our situation…I had to apologize to him for betraying his confidence.

I learned a hard lesson that day. I learned that not every person in my life needs to know every detail of my life. And that, even as I learn to love others with the huge love of Christ, I can guard my heart…that there truly is a wise way to love.

> This is my prayer: that your love will flourish and that you will not only love much but well. Learn to love appropriately.
>
> —Philippians 1:9 (MSG)

Apart

M Y HUSBAND AND I had been friends for a few years before we started dating. Pretty good friends. But it was safe, because we were both dating other people at the time. We probably talked on the phone every day for about a six-month time period (while dating others), went out to breakfast at the local pancake house from time to time, and, oddly, sponsored a Compassion child together (don't ask).

We started dating a few weeks after we went away to college (*different* colleges), and, of course, after we both had broken up with our current flames. It was a very sweet courtship at the beginning. I remember when he first offered me his arm to take while on a walk around Trinity (my alma mater). I remember when he first took my hand while on a walk around Olivet (his school). (I was a cheap date, I'm realizing...geez, Beth, hold out for a bit more than touring campuses of private colleges.)

About two or three months into the dating relationship, I noticed I was thinking about him all the time. We would talk a few times a day; we would call and let the phone ring only once so the other person knew we were thinking of them; we wrote letters; we sent care packages; we even audio-taped one-sided conversations and sent those to each other. I had an hourly countdown until I would see him again (there was sometimes a two-week stretch in between visits), and every hour, I'd cross off a number. Can anyone say *infatuation*?

Some may chalk this up to young love…but we started having problems in the spring…about five or so months in. And I became… ummm…*obsessed*. He was all I thought about. The potential demise of our relationship would send me into a tailspin. Things were not right in my world. Even though he wasn't on campus, I still didn't socialize all that much other than with my roommate and a few others, and my time with God was nil.

I remember grabbing my Bible one afternoon and heading out for a walk over by the pond on campus. I knew I needed to clear my head, I knew things weren't right, but I didn't know what to do about it. I did one of those open-the-Bible-to-a-random-page-and-let's-hope-God-speaks-through-something-meaningful things. Thankfully, He did. Here's what I read that day:

> I said to the Lord, "You are my LORD; apart from you I have no good thing."
> —Psalm 16:2 (NIV)

I remember this verse all these years later because it became real to me on a spring afternoon when I was in need of a word from God.

I had made Kevin my "good thing." My all-encompassing good thing. Friends fell to the wayside. Schoolwork was something that got done because it had to be done. And Jesus…well, I tried to fit Him in when I could. But in those moments, it hit me. If I were going to be walking apart from Jesus…and I was at the time and knew that I was… nothing in comparison would be good. I couldn't have Kevin as my one and only and just add Jesus to the top like icing. *Jesus* needed to be my one and only.

I walked back to the dorm with some new resolves. One, I was done calling Kevin…he could call me if he wanted to talk to me. Two, I was going to spend time with my friends. Three, and most importantly, Christ would become my priority.

I wish I could say this lasted for the rest of our courtship and completely revolutionized our relationship and how I handled life from that point on. But I was young. And stupid. And still in love. And life usually isn't like that anyway. If you think about it, don't we tend to spend the entirety of our lives relearning and reliving maybe a handful of lessons over and over again, just dressed up slightly differently each time?

But in that moment…I had been spoken to intimately, and I had responded. And I was not going to live *apart* anymore. Got any good things you need to shake out of first place?

Chapter 17

Power in the Path Not Taken

MY THEN BOYFRIEND/NOW husband, Kevin, and I became engaged during our Christmas break of his senior and my junior year in college. I was a happy girl. I was marrying a man that I had been able to laugh with and talk to for hours on end. I was marrying a man who I fought with, but looked at it as, *We must be so comfortable with each other that we can fight like this.* (I just want to pat myself on my twenty-year-old head when I think back to the me that I was then. Or give me a hug. Or a smack. I was so…~~stupid~~… *naïve.*)

Things were moving along, plans were being made. Like a freight train barreling down the tracks, there was no stopping me. My dream wedding had been planned since I was five apparently, just needing the small detail of the groom to insert and complete the picture. In about three months, everything for the most part was set…in stone. I even planned to take classes through the summer so I could graduate a semester early and get us married off in January instead of waiting until the following summer.

Then one fateful day, I was talking to one of my bridesmaids on the phone—my second step cousin, twice removed, we used to joke. She is a couple years older than me and is whip smart. I trusted her completely. So much so that she was who I chose to go to New York with for the weekend when my plans fell through with my original traveling companion because I knew I'd be super safe with her. So anyway, when she started grilling me on my upcoming marriage, you'd think I would've taken it in stride. Not so much. When she asked didn't I think we were too young to get married, I rattled off a list of reasons as long as my arm to the contrary. (I'm wondering now why that list was on the tip of my tongue…had I been trying to convince myself of the same thing?) We got off the phone on okay terms as I guess I had been able to convince her that I knew what I was doing.

Later that day, Kevin and I were on the phone and I was recounting my conversation with my inquisitive cousin. I said to him, "And then she said, 'don't you think you're too young to get married?' and I told her no… You don't think we're too young, do you?" Pause. (Warning: Men, this is not where you want to pause in a conversation.) "Wait a minute…do you think we're too young to get married?" My then-fiancé mumbled something about not being sure and I abruptly said, "I'm coming over," and hung up on him.

We lived about ten minutes away from each other, which was good, because I needed ten minutes to decide what I was going to say. I wish I could say I prayed through it. I think *seethed through it* is more like it. Because here's what I came up with (it's the stuff of movies, I'm tellin' ya). I walked in the front door, without knocking (I'd show him who's boss), (and can I just say, *Thank You, Jesus*, that no one else was home), and into the kitchen where he was sitting at the table. On the way over, I had taken my engagement ring off and put it back in the box. I slammed the ring box on the kitchen table and said, looking right at him (and pardon my French, in advance), "I don't want this damn thing back until you know what the hell you're doing with me." (Obviously not the prayed-through version.) Then I stormed out.

Is he coming after me?, I wondered as I quickly walked to my car. *If he loved me, he would*, I answered myself back. He didn't. He let me walk away. *Ouch.* I think I heard the sound of my heart breaking truly for the first time in that moment.

Fast forward through the gory details of undoing a wedding, getting a D in a psych course (in my major, for goodness' sake) because I was completely depressed and couldn't concentrate, driving on a whim to Iowa just to "get the hell out of town" only to turn back around in Ottawa (about forty-five minutes away) because it was back before cell phone days and I knew my mom would be worried, followed by a much needed break from our relationship. Needless to say, that was a long, hard summer.

During the fall, my last semester at college, I met a guy in my make-up-because-I-got-a-D-in-a-course-in-my-major class. Kevin and I were on tenuous terms. Half together, half not. My heart was his but also so was not. And this new guy sauntered in to my life. *Sauntered.* That's funny that I use that word because he's not really a sauntering kind of guy. But he was demonstrative. He told me I was beautiful more times in three months than I had heard perhaps in my entire life. He kept a journal, for heaven's sakes, and would occasionally read entries to me… *about me.* He was a good man and I fell for him quickly and hard.

He never kissed me. It's really one of those life regrets that we never did. And yet, so much might've been different if we had. I can look back on that time as sweet, pure, innocent. We didn't get entangled in anything…well, only emotions were entangled. He really helped to bring healing to me during that time. He didn't pounce on my vulnerability. He just was kind to me. And, did I mention, told me I was beautiful about a hundred times when I needed to hear it the most.

But the pull of what Kevin and I had was too much for me to bear. And one night, I told my friend that I was going back with Kevin and called Kevin and asked him if he'd take me back.

I have thought of the path not taken many, many times in the past fifteen or so years. There is no way at all for me to know that had I continued to see my friend, we would have begun officially dating and gotten married. I'm guessing no, but really, there's no way to know. And it's probably for the best that way.

But this is what I do know, despite the seemingly harder of the two roads that I chose…I am who I am because I married Kevin. (That can go a myriad of ways, like when Kevin says to someone, "It wasn't the same without you…" *Ummm, thanks?*) I am the mother of Sara Taylor and Jack Ryan because I married Kevin, and no one can tell me that they are my "wrong road" children. I became the Women's Ministry Director partly out of my loneliness and struggle in our relationship, which led to my job at church, which shaped the trajectory of my experiences and my life so much I can hardly believe it. I wrote my first book and then my second and then my third and now my fourth because I married Kevin, because of the stories that have come out of our life together. And that is a gift that my soul can almost not bear sometimes. And I met countless women because of the church he and I have attended for the entirety of our marriage…countless women who have shaped my life and become my sisters…some I haven't talked to in ages, but some who I am having dinner with tonight. And I cannot even fathom my life without my girls. No way are my current girlfriends my plan B girlfriends. *No way.*

Thinking about my path not taken has occasionally brought tears to my eyes, if I'm honest. Even though, really, there is no way to know how it might have turned out anyway. But the path I did take—the more challenging path…well, it ended up being the richest one I could ever take. The most beautiful one. The most loving one. And, really… truly, the one God wanted me on.

Chapter 18

Not Handling This All That Well

I CAN'T JOURNAL RIGHT now because I equate that brown striped notebook of mine with God. And right now I don't know what I should say to Him. Or ask Him. Or think about Him.

I had followed His leading in something ridiculously huge, scary, and scandalous, and *felt* His guiding clearly and *experienced* His peace profoundly. Even telling some friends the other night that "me and Jesus, we're like this these days" (crossing my two fingers together to illustrate our closeness). I knew, like deep, deep down knew, that I was doing what Jesus had led me to do.

And then two people put a kibosh on it. Really? That's how this works? I am a grown woman who is trying to follow God...*not* an immature woman who is trying to "follow her heart" all New-Agey style...and I am able to be told, *nope, sorry, you are basically wrong in your thinking. Yep, that must suck, but move along, Betty.*

You're kidding me, right? A month of prayer and reading and seeking wise counsel is just thrown out by two men who thought about the thing for a day. Okay, actually, one of them thought about it for all of five minutes before offering up his veto.

I've heard of dying to self, but this is on an entirely new level for me. I felt part of me die in that denial. My freedom was stepped on. My free will was taken away, so it seemed. I was told, in that sentencing, that I am an invalid part of this equation. Interesting, because I thought I am one of the key players in this equation…

What I would give right now to name names and rat some people out. How I'd love to spill details in black and white. How I'd give anything to clunk some heads together. Okay, so I'm dealing with some slight issues of bitterness. But you would be too. What thirty-eight-year-old likes to be told what to do by two, non-praying, unfamiliar-with-the-facts people?

And not just told what to do. That would've been one thing. But accused of only thinking of myself. Hmmm, that's why I spent a month thinking and praying about it? That's why the road I chose—of several non-easy roads to choose from in a pretty tough situation—is probably the hardest of them all. Because I am a glutton for punishment who wants to take everyone else down with me, apparently. Yes, that falls right in line with my character. I could see why they would think that.

I'm furious and devastated and beside myself. I am second-guessing my walk with Christ. *Didn't He lead me? Or was I deceived? Or did I just make something up that I wanted to hear? Or did He lead but I'm being disobedient in not standing up for this?* And I'm second-guessing my ability to make a decision for myself, any decision, let alone a hefty one.

So you know how I've handled myself so far in the past eighteen hours? I've taken two crying showers (you know the kind, where you just stand there letting the water run over you while sobbing uncontrollably). I've eaten upwards of a dozen cookies, along with my share of cookie dough, and nothing else so far today. I've barely journaled a page worth (which is pretty telling for me when I'm feeling the way I'm feeling). I've watched Regis & Kelly do their morning banter. I made dinner (at nine o'clock in the morning, for some reason). And I've Googled random celebrities that I haven't thought about in years. That is how I'm dealing with my current crisis. Hey, I didn't say I'd be giving you any solid steps to follow here. I don't go running into God's loving arms every time I fall, or am knocked down, though I'm getting better at that with time.

So what am I going to do now? My therapist told me to "get up, girl." I think I still need some more time on the couch.

Chapter 19

Ouch

I'VE BEEN THINKING about my interpersonal skills lately. Or lack thereof, I should specify. About my pathetically low patience level. About my excruciatingly high plane of self-absorption. About my intolerance for all things that bug me. And how I usually don't bother keeping my annoyances to myself. About when my job title at church was Director of Connection, how I used to joke with the staff that I would've loved to have the following motto on my business card: "I'll connect you, but I don't have to like you." And how I wish I were more than just half-kidding.

Don't get me wrong. I don't hate all people. I don't even think I hate any people at all. (I say this like I think I should get a pat on the back or something...look at me, everybody, I'm not a hater...*oooh.... ahhhh....bravo, Beth...*) And I'm really good with strangers and African children. They like me. Okay, not all strangers, but most strangers. In fact, I think I struggle with those I live with; I do pretty darn well with my closest girlfriends; I struggle with the next level a bit—people who kind of know me, or who think they know me; and then, like I said, I'm good with strangers and African children. But they probably only like me because most of them don't see white people all that often, let alone blondes...the African children, not the strangers...I'm sure most strangers have seen a blonde white woman before. But beggars can't be choosers, so I'll take what I can get.

I've been going round and round, via email, though I know better, with someone in my life who knows me *kind of*, who I went to for help on a pretty big problem, and who, best as I can tell, is running for "Christian most likely to kick someone while she's down." (Where do I vote?) Because I am getting emotionally beat up with every email I receive. As in, I hold my breath when I see that name on an incoming message, and then I end up crying through the entire reading of it. (Let me reiterate that I went to this person for *help*. Not a verbal and repeated slap in the face.)

I know I've got issues, don't get me wrong. But, man, I didn't realize I had so many. Or that they are so huge. Or so annoying. Or so personally offensive. It's as if unleashing on me has been a long-awaited moment. And so I'm trying to take it all in. I really am. I figure it's one of a few things going on here: a) Either this is rooted in anger over something from a long time ago, b) a minion of satan has been sent to destroy me, which I don't really believe, or c) truth is being spoken to me—it's just that it's unfortunately couched in harshness. If it's "c", I have promised myself not to throw the truth-filled baby out with the mean-spirited, ill-timed, inappropriate-venued bathwater. So I am availing myself to each accusation. Which, as you can imagine, has been a blast. Who among us likes to sit and recount all of our bad points, let alone knowing that it's not the Spirit bringing them to mind, but that it's coming from someone who is being driven so crazy by your imperfections that they are compelled to point them all out to you, one by one, through email? Yeah, me too.

But I'm trying to be mature. Well, maybe not totally mature. Otherwise I probably wouldn't be writing an essay about it, but *whatev*… it's my book…at least I'm not naming names. I'm asking Jesus to help me sift through each shortcoming, to look past the motives and the tone, and see what is truth and what I need to let go of.

So far, I'm still stinging from the pain. But my dear friend and mentor just told me to look at each thing while holding Jesus' hand. And know that if the intent were to hurt me or to condemn me, Jesus is not in it. That is not how He would do it. I'm trusting that He'll meet me here in my deep need, in my self-focused interrogation, and that gently…so gently, He'll point out where I could use some transforming.

But the best news is this: He is in charge of bringing any and all changes to completion. He's committed to the process, no matter how long it might take. It originates with Him, not with the accusers, or with my striving and trying harder. Maybe, just maybe, He'll soften hearts toward me, soften my heart toward others, and then remind me that His opinion of me is really the only one that matters anyway.

III

Once upon a time, there was a girl who...

...went to Africa and experienced God...

Chapter 20

Africa Called and I Answered

I T WAS MARCH 7, 2008—the morning I was leaving for Sierra Leone, Africa for the first time, when I had this conversation with my nine-year-old son, Jack:

Jack: I have one question for you.

Mom: Okay, go ahead.

J: Who said you had to go to Africa for ten days?

M: (thinking, thinking…) Well, honey, I really think Jesus wants me to go.

J: But did He say *Ten days*?

And that is how I left. Wondering myself, who told me to go to Africa? Why am I doing this? Am I insane? Going somewhere so far away? Leaving my kids for ten days? Going with people I barely know to a place I've only read about where I'll be eating who-knows-what-kind-of-food and bathing in who-knows-what-sort-of-conditions? Going when I really have no transferrable-to-African-culture skills? (What was I going to teach them—how to write a great email or put together a really cute outfit?) Basically, what was I thinking and had I really heard from God on this one?

I remember when I first gave my life to Christ…I clearly recall telling God twenty-three years ago that I'd do anything for Him, just *please don't send me to Africa* (whatever I thought Africa represented back then). I think I thought that to follow Him meant that He'd probably be asking me to do a bunch of stuff I wouldn't want to do, and I was drawing a line in the sand. *I give You all of me, but...* I can only imagine Him smirking each time I'd say something like that, Him knowing that twenty-plus years later, He'd end up working Africa into His little girl's heart and that I'd be begging for Him to orchestrate a trip for me to go on.

It surprised even me that I have become the kind of person to do what I just did, to go to a place so far away, so far removed from all I know and love. My former pastor and still good friend emailed me, in response to my trip recap letter:

"High maintenance diva + Africa = miracle of God."

Funny. Classic. *So very true.* How God has changed me and my heart and my life the past three years is almost unreal to me...at times, I barely recognize myself. And that's okay. It's more than okay actually.

There is no way to sum up Africa, but basically I would say that it is everything you would picture it to be—only with more poverty and more beauty, more sickness and more joy, more dirt and heat and more hope...just simply more real. I think we like to pretend that what we hear is going on over there isn't really going on over there. But it is. Not all children are in school; not all people eat even two meals a day; many people bathe in dirty, diseased water that they also must drink for lack of any other sources. People are dying for reasons they shouldn't be. The obstacles they face each day are huge, but so is their contentment, which blew me away.

So I'm left with the now-what questions. I've been reading about Africa for a couple years...I've been speaking and writing about it...I begged God to let me go...and I went. So now what? Well, I pray for an open heart, for my desire to learn about that place to continue to thrive, for God to live and move and breathe through me, and for Him to tell me what to do next...for ideas that are creative and smart and doable and yet just beyond my reach so I know God is in them. Because those kinds of ideas are the best ones. For Him to fill me up and then let me love others in adventurous ways until I'm completely tapped out... burned to the ground. In the best possible way.

Chapter 21

Jesus, I'm in Africa!

I'M NOT A big dreamer. What I mean by that is that I don't have many nighttime dreams. That I actually recall, that is. But a few days before I went to Africa, I had a pretty clear one. It lasted all of fifteen seconds really, but it was telling. And freaked me out.

I was all alone in a jungle, and I was running. I remember feeling scared but that everything was okay all at the same time. And I yelled out, "Jesus, I'm in Africa!" Now, I wasn't saying it like, "Woo hoo—look at me, Jesus! This is awesome!" I was saying it like, *Can You see me? Do You know I'm here? I'm scared to death!* And then I woke up. I'm not a huge fan of dreams like that.

The next morning I analyzed it to death. Is this God's way of telling me not to go? Am I going to be accidentally left behind in a jungle all by myself? Will I be kidnapped? Or simply, are those just normal fears of going being worked out in my subconscious?

I shared this with my therapist and she said, "Interesting that you didn't call out for Kevin or one of your girlfriends. Even in your dreams, you called out for Jesus." I breathed a happy sigh when she said that. My dream didn't need to mean anything except a reminder that I've got Jesus and He's got me, and when the rubber meets the road, He is who I count on, even deep, deep down.

That would come to mean a lot to me in the weeks leading up to the trip. I had just quit my job of four-and-a-half years, and due to a water pipe freezing and bursting in our home, my kids and I had been living in a hotel for over a month just before I was scheduled to leave. To say I was upended is an understatement. I felt so unprepared, in my heart *and* logistically, for Africa, it wasn't even funny. And I realized, looking back on that time before I left—seeing as a pipe bursting wasn't out of the reach of God's sovereignty—that maybe He wanted me to feel unprepared, so that I would count on only Him and none of my human devices to feel in control. Which I may tend to do from time to time.

And that's what happened. I went feeling nauseous and scared and so unready. But I went. And He met me time and time again in very little, private moments.

At one point, He woke me up in the middle of our flight from London to Senegal to witness the sun rising over Africa. And this is what I wrote in my journal:

"I'm in Africa. I'm not even on the ground yet. And we could still crash. Or I could be kidnapped and killed as soon as I get there. But I asked to come to Africa and You answered with both hands wide open. I'm not even on land but You let me come and my heart will never forget this gift. Thank You for loving me. Thank You for following me all the way out here! *Jesus, I'm in Africa!*"

Chapter 22

I Am Weak, but They Are Strong...

SOMETHING I'VE NOTICED about myself is that I tend to learn deep lessons from the tiniest things of life. It's the little moments, the snippets of conversations or a quote that I read, that can jump out at me and get stuck in my head and work their way into my heart.

In Africa, I had so many of those little moments that helped to shape me, but one that stands out happened when we were at the medical clinic. Four of us on the team were helping the head nurse dispense the drugs that the doctor had prescribed. (Frightening, I know. Apparently, in Africa, to become a pharmacist you simply need to be able to snap on a pair of those latex gloves.)

There was a nine-month-old baby who was prescribed these fairly big pills and the doctor had asked that we cut them in half. I was still surprised to see how large of a pill, even cut in half, that this baby was supposed to be able to swallow, so I asked the nurse if I should cut them into fourths. She said that the baby would be able to do it. I laughed and said that I wouldn't even be able to swallow them and she said, *"African children are stronger than you are."* She meant to be funny but we both knew how true that statement really is.

Throughout the afternoon, I said that line over and over again in my mind, and it hit me. I am not strong enough to live the life that the average African lives each day. In wondering why I have been "allowed the privilege" to be born in the United States, the answer came to me from an obscure place. It's because, in essence, I wouldn't have been able to *handle* those particular difficult circumstances.

However, I also realized that over the past few years, God has been making me strong enough to come alongside the people of Africa and serve them in many different ways both there and from home.

That one small sentence has challenged me and given me courage as I pray through what my personal next steps are for serving the people of Africa. And I was also reminded that Africa isn't a project for us to undertake...Africa is filled with people living their lives in very challenging circumstances, and I have the resources and capabilities to do something to help.

So I thank God that I live where I live, but I do so humbly, knowing that He chooses hardships lovingly and intimately based on our make-up. And in my gratitude, I look for ways to reach across the Atlantic with the love of Christ, doing so wisely and generously and unselfishly, hoping to follow God's leading. For when I am weak—and I *am* weak—then He is strong.

> One thing God has spoken, two things I have heard: that you, O God, are strong, and that you, O Lord, are loving. Surely you will reward each person according to what he has done.
> —Psalm 62:11-12 (NIV)

Chapter 23

A Phrase That I Hope Sticks

ONE OF THE gals on my Africa team was a twenty-one-year-old. She is a spitfire. She is so smart. She's going to change the world. Who am I kidding, she already is.

And she has a vocabulary all her own. She reminds me of the main character from the movie *Juno*. She says things like "hard core" and… okay, it's only been a month but I'm totally forgetting how she talks. I just know it was completely endearing. And she got me hooked on one of her words. A very out-of-character-for-me word.

Whatev.

Now, I had never heard this slang version of the word "whatever" before. Apparently it's even in a Verizon commercial, but I hadn't seen it. She didn't say it with adolescent apathy…it was more like, "that's life." And I loved it. Loved it so much, I came home saying it. Saying it so much that my eleven-year-old daughter is saying it and my husband is ready to kill me.

Now, *whatev* represents several things to me. It means a complete departure from my anal-retentive personality of caring about every single detail and every last duck being in a perfect little row. It means bringing the slower pace of Africa home with me, and that everything's going to be okay. It means growth…growing beyond what I've been used to. It means in the big picture of life, who cares really that the to-do list isn't going to get finished before our dinner party even though it was promised to be done before then? *Not me, I'm not going to care…whatev.*

But it also means something deeper. I've said *whatev* a thousand times in the past month—mostly in response to not getting my way on something very, very small. But I've noticed I've said it on a few really big, unnamable things too. As in, *cast your cares on the Lord and He will sustain you…whatev.* And, *do not worry about tomorrow because tomorrow has enough worries all its own…whatev.* And, *God's ways are higher than my ways…God's big enough to take care of this for me…pick up His light and easy yoke and give Him your burdens…God's love for me is overflowing and everlasting, so really, whatev.*

No adolescent apathy here…more like a mid-lifer's mantra. Whatever happens…really, *whatever happens*, it's all going to be alright. He promises. And my soul whispers, with a sigh and a smile, *Whatev.*

Chapter 24

The Last Night

FRANKLY, I'M HESITANT to write this down. It almost feels too intimate between me and God, even though there were another hundred and fifty people there when it happened. But again, I seem to not be able to not write it. So here goes.

On our final night in Africa, our partner church planned a going-away celebration for us. We thought it was going to be this little party at the house where we were staying. Turns out it was the final worship ceremony at the end of their pastors' retreat. They had purchased gifts for us—cool sandals and authentic African clothing. They had worked on special songs to perform for us. We had communion together (which I pounded back like a shot of tequila because I hadn't been paying attention when the plate came back around again). And it was outdoors, at night, and somehow they had orchestrated God creating a display of thunder and lightning that went on for at least an hour without one drop of rain falling on us. A-mazing.

And then there was the worship. These people know how to let go and let God, that's for sure. They close their eyes, they sing with all their might, they raise their hands and throw back their heads, they dance with great joy and bask in His Presence. Keep in mind when I say this that the majority of the people I was worshipping with are poorer than poor and eat perhaps one, maybe two, meals a day. And their great joy is nothing short of contagious. Even for a conservative, white, Midwestern girl like me.

And here's the moment. It's so simple and may very well mean absolutely nothing to you, which I understand and will not be offended by. But during the last song, people were up and dancing, and before we each knew it, we were being pulled up on our feet and into the center of the group. And with arms raised and no thoughts of self or heat or bugs or impending rain, I danced. I danced for God under a rumbling African sky with dark-skinned people who, in a week's time, I had grown to love and respect and envy, in the best sense of the word. And it lasted all of two minutes and I will never forget that feeling. Of feeling more like me than I had ever felt before. Of being connected to near-strangers who were family. Of not being self-conscious. Of being free. Of being on the other side of the world but feeling so very much at home all at the same time. And I closed my eyes and took it all in. And it was glorious. And I knew that I'd get to do that again one day.

Chapter 25

Jack's Second Question

A FTER I CAME home from Africa, I was sick for two days, but did laundry, checked email, got on with life. *Tried* to get on with my life. (How, really, do you just move on again after seeing all I saw? How do you go to the grocery store or think about buying yourself a new pair of shoes or plan a birthday party for your kid? *You don't*, is probably the only answer, but then again, you sort of just do.)

But I came back more prayerful. Okay, not even really praying *more*, though maybe I was. But praying more *deeply*. Maybe with a bit more power than I had before. A bit more purpose. At least I'd like to think I was. And I was trying to do that with my kids too. Wanted them to hear an intensity behind my prayers, an expectation that God really just might do the things I was asking for…what a concept.

One night, after reading a Bible story and praying for Jack, I was kneeling beside his bed, just giving him one last little squeeze, when he said, "I have a question."

Okay, last time he said that, he had me wondering if I were a horrible mother for going to Africa for ten days. Still, I didn't bolt out of the room or try to change the subject. "Okay."

"Tell me how to hear Jesus the way you heard Him tell you to go to Sierra Leone."

Whoa.

Here's what I said. I talked about having a quiet time each day, reading the Bible on your own, praying, asking Jesus to talk to you, asking for adventures.

I don't know if that answer were satisfactory to his nine-year-old curious heart. I think what he really wanted to know, which were probably hard for him to articulate, was, "Do you really actually hear Jesus talking to you? And if so, really, Mom…how do you get Him to do that?" Like it's a magic trick or something. *Well, honey, you put the rabbit under a hat and then, voila, you too can hear Jesus.*

I was recounting this story to a friend a week later who was in the middle of deciding, with her husband, if they should up and move their family to another state for a job offer. And she said, "Yeah, can you tell me that too?"

I just mumbled something about barely knowing how to explain it to a nine-year-old let alone to another thirty-seven-year-old and we kinda laughed and moved on.

But this is something people want to know. Heck, He actually *does* talk to me from time to time, and I still want to know how it happens. How did I know Jesus wanted me to go to Sierra Leone? That was more of a circumstantial leading for me. I wanted to go. I asked God to let me go. Okay, truth be told, I begged God to let me go. A trip came up as a possibility, but it seemed far-fetched…during the school year, ten days, are you kidding me? I didn't think it would work logistically. But another gal who was planning to go just said to me, "I've been trying to think of ways all morning for you to go on that trip." And I thought, *geesh, if she could be thinking of ways for me to make it work, I guess I can do that much.* So I thought a little bit (wasn't that hard of a solution after all) and I talked to my husband and he said yes. And there you have it. But that's not always how God leads me.

He does sometimes talk to me. I wish it were more often. I wish I would shut up more so He can get through. Sometimes it's an impression of a phrase or two, like, "I love you." Sometimes, like a conversation we had yesterday afternoon, God went on for several minutes as I felt Him speak truth after truth after truth over me…things I desperately needed to hear from Him…things I was scared to admit I needed healing in.

Sometimes, He has actually told me to go to a certain place, and it not even be a quote unquote spiritual thing. One particular time happened over ten years ago but I remember it like it was last week. My husband and I had bought our first little home. Little isn't the right word. You could stand in the middle of it and "spit in any direction" as Kevin used to say. It was teeny tiny. But it was ours and I loved it. I painted the front door red and we hung flower boxes on the windows. I was in heaven.

One day I decided to put wallpaper border up in our bathroom. Southwestern. Back when southwestern was in. Back when I didn't know that you didn't have to like something just because it was "in." I bought cacti statues and everything for this little bathroom of ours. I sponge-painted the walls in light peach and light green. Oh my word, this is sounding absolutely horrifying. It really was cuter than the image I'm conjuring up for you, I promise. (At least I think it was.) So, my last step was the wallpaper border. We didn't have a lot of money, but I was feeling like God wanted to bless me with southwestern wallpaper border, with light peach and light green as the main colors. I seriously felt that.

(He and I were in a very sweet stretch of walking very closely together. Mainly because of three things: one, I had finally relented to getting baptized and felt such a smile of God on my life after that step of obedience, it was almost unreal. Two, I had just taken a part-time job at church after months of not working and trying to "find myself"...i.e. after months of shopping with no money, and wasting my time in chat rooms and watching TV. And three: He and I were spending an awful lot of time together and it was just wonderful. So, yes, we were so close that I felt He wanted to give me wallpaper border.)

So, I started driving to a place that I thought would maybe carry wallpaper border. I didn't go to Kmart or Target or Bed, Bath & Beyond, drove right past them in fact. I'm not sure why really, other than I had this inkling, for lack of a better word, that I was *supposed* to go to this home décor place that wasn't even all that close to my house. I drove to where I thought it was. It wasn't there. As I was nearing a stoplight, I was going to make a turn so I could just head home, when I felt God tell me, "Keep going...it's up past the next light, on the right." Keep in mind, I'd never actually been there before…I had maybe driven by a few times in as many years. Couldn't even tell you the name of it. But I thought, *what have I got to lose? I've already driven this far.* So I kept driving.

Let's just say, the still, small voice of God is more reliable than MapQuest. Okay, really bad analogy. Because my *cat* is more reliable than MapQuest. This one's more accurate: God is more reliable than the British woman on my GPS who tells me to exit in five meters. Because sure enough, I look up and realize that just past the next light, on the right, is that home décor store. Now, I must admit, I was giddy with anticipation at this point. God had just told me where a store was located. I couldn't wait to get in there.

I am not making this up. I walked into the store and the first thing I came to was a table of "everything's 50% off." On the very top of the middle bin looking me right in the eye was my holy grail…southwestern wallpaper border with light peach and light green, FIFTY PERCENT OFF. I picked it up, walked to the counter, paid for it, and floated home. God loved little ol' me so very much that He wanted my goofy looking bathroom to look just right.

So maybe when Jack's just a little older, I'll tell him this story and I'll end with, "Yes, Jack. I really do hear Jesus talk to me. And I do it by listening. And letting Him love me." So simple. So amazing. I want more.

Chapter 26

Angels in Africa

THIS IS A true story that was told to me second-hand. But I want to stress that the person who told it to me can be trusted. (I guess I should also stress that so can I.) Don't let the fact that this is a second-hand story, now technically third-hand I guess, take away from the weight of it. Pretend the main character is telling you this story, because I don't want you to miss out on the chills.

My friend told me of a time when he was in Nigeria a few years ago. An American friend of his was also in Nigeria at the time and recounted a situation that had recently happened to him. Okay, this makes it fourth-hand. Still true, though.

He was driving along one day and saw that a car was careening in his direction, headed right toward his driver's side. This man knew in that moment that he was about to die, so he just yelled, "Jesus!" and shut his eyes tightly, gripping the wheel.

A few moments later, when he realized he was still alive, he opened his eyes and looked out his window to see the bumper of the other car an inch away from his car. But he also noticed something opaque between the two cars.

He looked out his car window and saw a thirty-foot angel. (Yes, I just said he saw a thirty-foot angel.)

He was sharing this with a native Nigerian friend later, sort of in an "I know I'm crazy...please don't tell anyone I told you this" kind of way, and the native Nigerian said, "Oh yeah, we have angels all over the place here."

Wow. I have nothing to add to this story, I just thought it needed to be told.

Chapter 27

Fake Rocks and Real Moments

IKNOW A WOMAN who travels extensively, taking weeks off at a time to discover a new part of the world that she's never been to before. She keeps a bowl of rocks, regular rocks, that she finds in each destination, and then writes their origin on them with a sharpie.

I loved that idea, so when I was in Haiti two summers ago, my first real exotic trip (a cruise to the Bahamas just doesn't cut it), I spent some time on the beach looking for just the perfect rock to bring home with me. I have one picture of me on that trip, taken by my traveling companion from Samaritan's Purse—it's a picture of me, alone, in the dark. I could be standing anywhere. I could be in Michigan for all anyone would know. I can't believe I have no pictures of me actually interacting with actual Haitians. But I have my rock! One that I realized as soon as I put it in its special place of honor could have been found at the local playground, again, for all anyone knew. But *I* knew I had gone there and experienced it and found that rock there. I had that souvenir, if you will, to commemorate that life-altering trip.

I found a rock in Africa too. On a dirt road as we traveled to a village in the jungle. We had to stop because one of our team members was feeling carsick and needed to throw up. Then the men decided that while we had stopped, they'd go use the jungle as a restroom. Needless to say, I went looking for rocks up and down the path while waiting for all the men to stop acting like savages. (Little did I know that the jungle would be our only restroom option for the remainder of the day…) I have an actual picture of me with my treasured rock, shifting it from one hand to the other. I made sure to put it in my suitcase as soon as we got back to the guesthouse and, lo and behold, it is nowhere to be found. But I have a picture of me with an African rock in my hand. I again wanted something from that place in my home as a constant reminder. So you know what I did? This is so lame. I actually went to my yard and got a rock, just yesterday, two months after my trip, and wrote in sharpie "Sierra Leone 2008", and placed it next to my Haiti rock. I thought to myself, *no one will ever know*. Except me. (And now you.)

But it got me thinking how we commemorate special moments. We spend thousands of dollars on wedding photographers and videographers, we have parties for graduations, we get presents for birthdays, we send cards to friends and loved ones on various holidays…we want to remember things. I recall right before my wedding, when I had gotten about as hyper as I could in the midst of the final preparations, somehow reminding myself that the time of my wedding to reception (about six or seven hours total) would be the same measure of time as any ordinary day. It wasn't going to pass in slow motion just because the event was above and beyond ordinary, just because I wanted it to last longer. The six or seven hours would still feel like six or seven hours, no matter what I did to slow it down, capture it, remember it.

And I've been thinking about God's view of time and of events. How we tend to elevate one moment above another but how, as He looks down on everything from before creation to the end of time… how time looks all the same to Him. The day of our birth and the day we went to traffic court are all the same in His eyes. Not that each day is boring or meaningless; I actually mean the opposite. Each day is a gift. Each day that is normal is a gift. I wrote in my journal the other day, "I thank You for this day even though I'm sad." It's important for me to acknowledge each and every day, and really, each and every moment, as one that has been granted to me, to be thankful for, to be celebrated, commemorated, remembered. Whether I'm quitting a job in a certain moment, or watching my cat walk across the patio sheepishly with a bird in its mouth (though this is probably more of a gift for my cat than, say, me…or the bird…), or planning my son's tenth birthday party, or writing another chapter in a book, or making dentist appointments, or sitting outside and "doing nothing"...they are all gifts. Gifts given to us by Someone who is crazy about us...Someone who, as Psalm 145:16 says, is "generous to a fault...who lavishes favor on all creatures."

So, when I was picking out my fake African rock yesterday, I grabbed one more to add to my collection. And I took my sharpie and this is what I wrote on it: **Here. Now.**

Because this place in this time is worth celebrating and remembering and basking in too.

Chapter 28

1 + 1 + 1 + 1 + ... = More Than Enough

RECENTLY A FRIEND said to me, "I look at the enormity of the problem and I can't help but think, 'what can one person do?'" It's occurred to me that I used to think that way too, but not anymore. One person can do so very much.

One person can pray with all she's got, begging God to intervene in any given situation, to pour out His power, to give her wisdom to know what she can and should do.

One person can give of her time in a way that will be a sacrifice to her and of great benefit to others.

One person can give money...even a little bit of money...and that can be added to what others have given and then multiplied when God steps in.

One person can call attention to an issue that is usually talked about in hushed tones...making people aware of something they may have had no idea about or have been trying to avoid.

One person can enter into the darkness, carrying her little bit of light, and shed great illumination where only dim shadows tend to dwell.

One person can touch another person's life in small ways—with a kind word, a gentle touch, a moment of time to listen and hold and cry with.

One person can take her gifts and pour them out into someone else's life, knowing that freely has she received and freely should she give.

One person can take her hurt and ask Christ to turn it into a blessing as she connects with the pain of another hurting heart.

One person can move into another person's life in large ways—with a shout against injustice, a rallying of a group to do something of meaning, a hand reaching out to draw someone out of their circumstances permanently.

As Beth Moore said on *Wednesdays with Beth,* "Helping just one person may not seem like much of a contribution. But to that one person, it's everything. *Everything.*"

This day, this moment, can be the day and moment that we allow our one life to do a world of good for someone else's life. What can one person do in comparison to the vastness of our world's problems? Each one of us can do much. We each have so much to give.

We have to just keep walking. Plant that seed. That's all we're responsible for. The harvest...what comes of it all...is not up to us. We can't see what's going on, really, every time we pray a prayer, every time we hold the hand of someone who is lonely, every time we fly to the other side of the world, every time we hug our child or share our hearts or commit a verse to memory or wipe a tear away or bring someone a meal or gently tell someone the hard truth or say we're sorry...nothing we can see. But when we see no result or when we feel like all we've got to give is nowhere near enough, I have a feeling that's when the biggest victories are being won in the spiritual realm. That's when the biggest love is stepping in to fill in the gaps.

> Pure and lasting religion in the sight of God our Father means that we must care for orphans and widows in their troubles.
>
> —James 1:27 (NLT)

IV

Once upon a time, there was a girl who...

...looked outside and saw God...

Chapter 29

Gratitude in Action

I AM WRITING FROM my new spot…my new morning spot, overlooking the pond that is in the forest preserve attached to our new property. I'm in awe of this place, of the beauty, of this gift. What a blessing I don't deserve.

I recently read of people in Nairobi who stake their claims at the tops of garbage heaps at the local dump, and *live their lives there* so no one takes their precious and coveted spots. And yet somehow…*somehow…* this beautiful, opposite-of-a-garbage-heap is my spot. Those people eat out of that heap, finding their sustenance there. They are punctured by tossed-away AIDS-infected hospital hypodermic needles on that heap. They guard that heap. They die on that heap. Real people do this. Real people, just like you and me, who have no other choices.

I will, more than likely, never go hungry, never get AIDS, never catch something from drinking contaminated water, not die hopelessly, purposelessly, lonely, hungry, desperately ill, or on a heap of anything, let alone garbage. I will live and die with more than I could ever need or want—a life of undeserved abundance.

To those who are given much, much is expected. *Much.* I've been given much, no doubt about it. Much is therefore expected of me. Am I, as an individual, thanking God with my life? Am I living richly toward others? Am I giving much, giving sacrificially, doing all that is expected of me and then some, praying ferociously, looking for God in the eyes of every person that comes my way?

At my new home, I have eighty-three trees in my yard (my "addition whiz" son counted for us the other day). *Eighty-three.* Some have a garbage heap to call their own, if they're counted among the lucky ones to get there first. And I have been given eighty-three trees just for my pleasure. I don't for a moment pretend to understand the why behind that paradox of pursuing.

But what am I doing with my life, Jesus? Am I grateful? Do You feel thanked? Am I doing the "much" that is expected of me? How can I love You back? Keep chipping away at my selfish heart. I want to thank You with my life. I ask these questions, though not as often as I should. And I am not always thrilled with the response that I feel comes my way.

We live, you and I, in the top three or so percent of the economic world. What in the world are we doing to say thank You to the One who has purposely placed us here for His pleasure and ours?

(For some cool ways to serve your community and the world, go to my website at www.elisabethcorcoran.com and click on the link on my homepage.)

Chapter 30

The Holy Spirit Just May Know What He's Talking About

HAVE YOU EVER felt God tell you to do something and you chose to not follow the leading? Well, this is a story of one of those times when I clearly felt God tell me something and I totally blew Him off. And then paid for it dearly.

My then nine-year-old daughter had been invited to a friend's house for a slumber party to celebrate her birthday. Though I had met this girl at her school, I had never met her parents. Red flag number one. But Sara really wanted to go, so I said yes.

When I dropped her off, I met only the father of the birthday girl as her mother was working the night shift. He seemed nice enough, but still, red flag number two. They also had two big dogs. Can't really call that a red flag, I just don't like big dogs. So that was maybe a pink-ish flag.

As I was getting in my van, I felt nauseous. I was literally feeling what I now realize was most definitely the Holy Spirit saying to me, *Go back and get her. Don't worry what anyone thinks. Bring her home.* Bright red flag. Flashing neon red flag. But this is the part of the story where I wish I had done something else but really did the wrong thing. Basically I said to myself or the Spirit or whoever's voice I was trying to convince myself I was hearing that *no, I am not going to get her…this is silly. She'll be fine…I just need to work on letting her go.*

Fast forward a few hours to about ten pm. I'm getting into bed and I'm not kidding when I say that I felt the Spirit, as clear as day, impress upon me, *Call over there and say you're going to pick her up.* To which I reply, *It's ten o'clock. I'm not calling there and I'm not going over there.* Don't think I bothered telling myself she was fine because by now, I was so torn up inside it wasn't even funny.

I fought to sleep, but only barely, when the phone rang at about eleven-thirty. Kevin came up to tell me he was going to get Sara because she called asking if she could come home. She claimed she wasn't feeling well so no one would make fun of her. Turns out she was scared. Mainly because they were watching "Scary Movie 3." You know the one—that parody of about ten other actual scary movies with a ton of profanity and scary masks and fake blood that nine-year-olds may not know is fake and some toplessness, apparently. (I'm sick just remembering this…)

I told Sara the next morning that I was so sorry…that I had felt the Holy Spirit telling me to come and get her. She said it was okay but she did then say this, "Why didn't you listen?"

Ouch. Why hadn't I? God, through His Spirit, was revealing His love for my daughter and for me, and I squelched it. I promised her and myself that I wouldn't make that mistake again.

Chapter 31

On My Knees

THE OTHER MORNING, the first thought that popped into my head as I started to wake up was, "on your knees." *Hmm...that's odd,* I thought. *Ummm, Jesus, if this is You, I'll get on my knees during my quiet time with You in just a bit.* (Yes, that's what I said to Jesus. Nice, huh?) It felt like a good compromise seeing as a) it seemed like an odd request, b) I wasn't sure if it were even Him telling me that, and c) I had a few things on the agenda and needed to get going with my day.

Fast forward about two hours and I was sitting down for my quiet time. I did, in fact, get on my knees, next to the bed, opening my hands up in a symbolic surrendering of myself and my day. Then I sat back down in the chair with my tea and immediately felt, "on your knees." *Okay, I just got on my knees. Didn't You just see me do that?* I asked, with a bit of attitude, as in *what more do You want from me?* "On your knees, in your heart," said the gentle Voice. *Oh. Now that's different. Wait... Jesus, am I holding something back from You that I don't know about?* My feelings were almost hurt, like when you proudly show your parents a hard-earned B and they ask why you didn't get an A. *Okay, I literally have to go now, but we'll talk about this again. Soon.*

He's been doing that to me more lately. The whole talking-to-me thing. There are a few reasons why that I can humanly point to in an attempt to explain it. For instance, there's a certain author that anytime I read something he's written, this happens. And I've upped one of my spiritual disciplines that I had let go of for awhile. And I just decided to take the plunge and lead a mission trip to Liberia. Things like that. But then there's the part that can't be explained. The holy part. The part that I have nothing to do with.

I had been out of town when I first heard the request…the command…the beckoning… of "on your knees, in your heart." And it followed me back home. I was putting laundry away and thinking about what was on my to-do list. What was on that to-do list included something I'm kind of embarrassed about…to finish up watching season one of a show I have recently become ever-so-slightly obsessed with. And as I was thinking to myself, *ooo, I'll do that next*, I heard "on your knees, in your heart," and I thought to myself, *surely You're not asking me to give that up…I'm almost done, and it's a harmless show.* So I pushed on past that Voice and watched it. And enjoyed it very much, thank you. Except for the guilt that was lingering over me. See, I don't always listen.

But why wouldn't I want to? Why wouldn't I want to listen to the Voice? Why wouldn't I want to do what it says, when it's never once led me astray and always has my absolute best interest in mind? When it's a Voice that is filled with love for me and driven solely by love?

One morning before a speaking engagement, during my quiet time, I asked what I should read…I told God I could use a little comfort, but what I really wanted was the passage He led me to years and years ago right before another speaking engagement when I was pretty scared, something about a congregation, but I didn't want to ask for that because I didn't actually believe He'd lead me to it and I didn't want to be disappointed when He didn't come through. Again, nice, right? So, I stuck with asking for comfort and He led me to Psalm 23: "Your rod and your staff, they comfort me" (23:4 NIV). And then my eyes drifted to Psalm 22, *on the same page*: "I will declare your name to my brothers; in the congregation I will praise you (22:22 NIV)." *Whoa.* That was the exact confidence-building verse from years ago that I had hoped to run across. Really…*whoa.*

So the other day, when I was thinking about a person I know who needed some extra cash for a project, I asked Jesus if He wanted me to help out and if so, how much. The amount that came to my mind was weird. Until I realized that the amount that came to mind was the amount that matched a check I had recently gotten. I thought, *really, Lord? Seriously?* And even though I doubted this ever so slightly, I figured I'd rather err on the generous side. Especially because as I signed the back of the check, I heard, "on your knees, in your heart."

Take some time today…not this week, not at your women's retreat next month, but today. Right now, even. And listen for the Voice of the One who loves you and wants to pour out His love and compassion over you. Today. In this moment. Just listen.

Chapter 32

The Next Right Thing

WHEN MY DAUGHTER was about six, we were driving down the street and saw a man standing on the corner holding a sign that read, "WILL WORK FOR FOOD." My daughter had just started to read, so she read his sign out loud and then asked me what it meant.

I told her that it meant that he didn't have money to buy lunch, which meant he didn't have a job, and maybe didn't have a place to sleep. There was a McDonald's right up the street and we weren't in any hurry, so I went through the drive-up and ordered that man some lunch. I drove back around the block, slowed down at the light, and handed him the lunch through my passenger side window. I never said a word about it, and neither did Sara.

I wasn't thinking that we were in the middle of some huge teachable moment. I was just doing "the next right thing," as I've heard it called. But the Spirit was at work, as He usually is, even when we're not giving Him a second thought.

Six or so months went by and we happened to be driving by that same corner. The homeless man wasn't even there, but my Sara said, "Mommy, do you remember when you gave that man some lunch?" I got chills. I could not believe that she remembered that, let alone from what seemed like so long ago, and without the visual reminder of the man himself standing there. So I just said, "Yes, honey, I remember."

Then my six-year-old said, "Mommy, that was so generous of you." (I didn't even know she knew what "generous" meant...)

What cost me five bucks and maybe ten minutes of my life planted a memory in my daughter's mind and now, thanks to the Spirit, into her heart that I never could have orchestrated. That when God loves us, we want to love others. Sometimes it costs a lot, and sometimes, nothing at all. And I had just been living my life...

Chapter 33

For Someone with Such a Freakishly Small Esophagus, You Have an Awfully Big Mouth

THIS IS A story of a time when I was sarcastic. (Wait, you're thinking, I thought all of the stories were about that.)

A couple years ago, I was sitting on my front porch on my sweet, little bench. Okay, sitting is painting a grander picture of me. I was undoubtedly sprawled out, unladylike, with the latest issue of *Glamour*. It was a gorgeous late spring day and I was being my typical lazy self.

Down the street came running a friend of mine. Running as in jogging…exercising. The opposite of lying on a bench with a magazine. I was so proud of her. This was before I started running and I just remember thinking things like, "That is so cool. You go, girl." However, I don't have that filter in my head that keeps me from saying inappropriate things. So instead of cheering her on, I said this…make that, I yelled this:

"YOU MAKE ME SICK!"

To which she turned, smiled, laughed, waved, and kept running.

You make me sick?! Wow, Beth, could you be any more encouraging? I was beside myself. That was so not what had been in my head.

Immediately I ran to my computer and shot her an email:

"I am so sorry about what I yelled at you when you were running. I can't believe I said that! Because this is what I was thinking—I was so proud of you, and it's so awesome that you run, and I wish I were more like you. Please forgive me, my friend." And I might have signed it, *Your dork of a neighbor.*

A few hours later, I got this reply:

"First of all, I knew the moment you said it that you'd be mad at yourself for saying it. And secondly, I knew that was your backwards way of encouraging me. No biggie...we're fine."

Now, I knew that she knew me well enough to know that I was being silly/stupid/sarcastic. I didn't really think she'd be angry with me over that comment. But...but I didn't want our most recent interaction to be *that.* So, it took me all of thirty seconds to fix it. I'm so glad I did.

I've gotten myself into situations much bigger than that...where I didn't choose the high road. I have lost friends over things that I didn't choose to fix. When I didn't choose love. I have lost friends over things someone didn't choose to fix with me. I can think of a few right now. My hope is that I won't let hard conversations get in my way anymore. The fear is not worth the loss.

Chapter 34

The Least I Can Do Is Often More Than Enough

WHEN I SENSE God nudging me to do something, sometimes I can actually feel my heart start to beat faster. This is happening to me more often lately, and it doesn't even have to be a huge thing, but I've learned that when I get that feeling, I'd better buckle up and do as He says.

One evening, my husband and I were having an overnighter away from the kids. We had just gone to a movie and were going to swing by a grocery store to pick up some snacks before heading to our hotel. I noticed a homeless man who had set up a makeshift bed at a storefront across the street. I got that feeling I was telling you about and asked Kevin as we walked into the store if I could pick up a few things for him. So while Kevin looked for chips and pop, I raced the aisles trying to pick out just the right things. It felt important. It felt like, *this could be his only meal for days…get this right, Beth.* I grabbed a bottle of orange juice, a bottle of water, a couple bananas and apples, I think, a deli sandwich probably, and a pack of gum.

I was excited and nervous as we got back in the car and Kevin drove us across the street. I got out of the van and walked over to the man, handing him the bag of food, with a short note inside that simply said, "Jesus loves you." I think I just said something like, "This is for you. I hope you have a good night." Something lame. What do you say to a man who doesn't have food, water, or shelter, when you do have all these things and so much more? You tell him to have a good night apparently.

As we drove away, I felt…deflated. He said thank you and I'm sure he was grateful, but I just felt like *really, Beth, was that the best you could do?* I was angry with myself. Which is pretty weird because most people probably just drove by him. *I've* driven by the "hims" of the world before, plenty of times.

I had tears in my eyes and silently prayed, "Jesus, send someone to help him, please…" And Jesus kindly whispered back, "I just did."

Chapter 35

The Writing Life

I REMEMBER MY SIXTH grade teacher's advice like it was yester-day...*keep writing.* She was *one of those* teachers. The kind that doesn't blend in with all the others. The kind that stands out as the one who saw something in me. I had just written my version of a Sweet Dreams novella. I was *obsessed* with Sweet Dreams romances. It was the early 80s. I hadn't discovered fashion or boys, really. (Well, except for Mark Miller. But he had discovered my best friend, so I had some time on my hands.) I couldn't get enough of those Sweet Dreams paperbacks that were all about the plight of the high school girl finding love, almost losing love through some precarious could-only-happen-in-a-teeny-bopper piece of fiction, and then triumphing with love (and the gymnastics medal or class presidency or some other also-coveted prize) at the end. And so I wrote one of my own. Okay. Clarification. I wrote one chapter. Something about going shopping at the mall and wondering if anyone would notice that my main character hadn't shaved her legs. It was, as best as I recall, a simply mortifying piece of work. But I wrote it. And I gave it to Mrs. Markowitz. And she told me it was good and to keep writing.

Now, that wasn't the first piece I'd ever written. I had started with poems, my first one pecked out on my Grandma's typewriter in her den when I was eleven. Now that was a masterpiece. It centered on "seagulls circling above me...as if doing their own little dance." Because we're told from day one to write what we know. And what eleven-year-old girl from

Illinois doesn't know her share of seagull tales? But wow, I remember the opening line of my first piece of work from over twenty-five years ago…shows you how profound stumbling upon your calling can be.

I moved on from that day, becoming the vice president of my local Archie and Jughead Comic Book chapter, which consisted of just me, and winning a writing contest where I described in detail my pure devotion to Betty and Veronica and the fan club that I led, which, by the way, was all lies, but that was before my morality kicked in. And my writing life blossomed from there. The occasional published poem in no-one-ever-heard-of publications. Including two bizarre ones I wrote on a bet/dare for my junior college newspaper to prove that the weirder the work, the better the odds of publication. I scored with my ode to spaghetti. Those art snobs.

Until one day, well after college and well into the baby-making years, I landed my first magazine article. In a no-one-ever-heard-of publication, but beggars were not going to be choosers on that day. I ran outside with the magazine in hand, a baby on my hip, a byline waving in the wind, to show my husband. I had been published! That was a glorious day. That was the first in many small moments when I whispered to myself, *I'm a writer.* But I'd say it to myself like, *But don't let anyone hear you say that!*

I wasn't ashamed of the calling, so why the hiding? Because, from what I can tell, I didn't trust it. Being a writer isn't like, for instance, being a waitress or an accountant or a librarian. You can't just apply at a place and get a job with a salary, benefits, and sometimes a cute uniform. Nope. You pretty much have to convince *life* that you are a writer. You have to fight against convention and art snobs and harsh critics and the inner voices that are typically filled with doubt and fear. I had barely convinced myself that writing was going to not just be how I figured out my life, but how I wanted to make my life…to make a living…before I started getting mail saying that I didn't really know what I was talking about, in the form of rejection letters. That I must've misunderstood the call. I used to love getting mail before that.

When I wrote my first book and began the process of finding a publisher, which let me say just might be one of Dante's seven rings of hell, I had no idea what I was up against. It's politics and who you know and getting a foot or hand or kneecap in the door. It took me, and I am not kidding, six weeks to write my first book. But it took me thirteen long, tortuous, testing-my-fortitude and commitment-to-my-supposed-blankety-blank-calling-and-who-said-I-wanted-to-be-a-writer-anyway months and fifty-two (yes, *fifty-two*) rejection letters before a publisher came knocking on my door. But a publisher did come. And the day I received my box of books in the mail was one of the best days of my life, and not just because it sort of redeemed the postal system for me, although that *was* huge.

I have gone on to write another one and self-publish. To write a monthly column for over eight years now. To write a third book, still looking for a publisher. And now this book, which I must've found a publisher for, because you, someone I don't know personally, is reading it.

I had asked a writing friend of mine for advice. This gal is several years ahead of me in the writing life, with five or six books under her belt. She's funny and humble and is always gracious and generous with her help and wisdom. I had quit my job and sat down to write whatever came to mind only to find an entire book on the tip of my tongue and I asked if she'd read it. The long and short of it was this. She asked me if I considered myself a writer, and when I said something like, "I haven't really thought about it lately, what with the job and the kids and such…", she said, "Well, you just quit your job, right? And your kids are both in school full-time? And you've published two books, have one waiting in the wings, and you just wrote another one in under a month? Beth, I think you're a writer."

But let me share with you maybe the best thing anyone has ever said to me about my writing. I just picked up again Anne Lamott's *Bird by Bird,* her wonderful guide on how to be a writer. I had read this the first time a few years ago and this is what I wrote up at the top of one of the pages: "January '04—I could read this writing every day. When I get to heaven, I'm going to write like her." And then I followed it with this: "(Pause) God speaking: 'When you get to heaven, you're going to write like *you*…only better.'" Sweet pursuit.

So to Mrs. Markowitz and Keri Kent (and all my other encouragers along the way—the staff of Archie & Jughead, the editors at the Joliet

Jr. College newspaper, circa 1989, the publisher of *Joyful Woman* magazine, to my Grandpa Klein who made copies of my first book at Kinko's to hand out to his Florida condo friends, to the great people of Kregel, to my friends who read my work and tell me they love it... and I'm sure I'm leaving a ton out), and to God, thank you and thank You. Thank you for agreeing with the quiet call I felt all those years ago sitting at my Grandma's typewriter and for pushing me on to more and better words.

Chapter 36

God vs. Evil

MY HUSBAND SENT me an email from work this morning linking me to a news article that reported on Steven Curtis Chapman's adopted five-year-old daughter being killed yesterday, run over accidentally by her older brother in their driveway. Now, I don't know Steven and Mary Beth Chapman, but my husband and I considered adopting last year and watched the informational video they put together. That, along with years of hearing his music on the radio, makes me feel like I kind of know him, I guess. Because this loss of theirs has me swinging back and forth from crying to sighing to looking off into space to trying to do normal things around the house and then back to crying again.

It kind of feels like the Church just got a collective kick in the gut. Seeing it online and then hearing it on two radio stations this morning, it kind of feels like the Christian version of 9/11 to me. Because if this doesn't have evil written all over it, I don't know what does. And I don't mean for one second that her big brother set out to do this. That's actually my point. Could it get more twisted than an innocent, loving older brother having to carry the burden of this for the rest of his life? It's as if the enemy has been watching this sweet family attempt to bring light into this dark world through music and illuminating the cause of adoption and he didn't like it one bit and thought he'd send one loud-and-clear message. *Well, we got it. You're real. And you've come to steal and kill and destroy. We get it.*

I was flipping channels this morning and I landed on a dark-skinned man talking in a bit of an accent and I had the vague idea, just by that quick first impression, that he was an African man in Africa, describing a war that he had witnessed. He was pointing to the classroom where some women and children hid, and he said, "The reason you will not find any bullet holes in the walls of this school is because the weapon of choice was a machete." I hear something like that and turn off the television. My heart cannot take stories of pain that are as real and deep as that. Some days I sit with the pain of this world, but most of the time I just have to make myself act like it really doesn't exist because how would any of us get anything done, get through even one day of living regular life, if we really, really let the state of our world sink in all at once. Don't tell me we don't have an enemy.

But back to the Chapman family. I can't imagine their pain. I can't imagine being targeted like that. Someone hating me so much that they would do something so horrible to me or my family. But then I remember, oh yes…lest I forget…their enemy is my enemy and he's more real than I give him credit for. I think one of the biggest tragedies of the Church today is not that we act like there's a devil behind every bush, but that we act like our enemy either isn't real or isn't all that hateful or we aren't making enough waves for him to come after us. But make no mistake, he is real and he is hateful and we are making waves.

But I don't want to leave you scared or, oh I don't know, *put off*, uncomfortable, maybe, by all this talk of a real enemy. I mean, I'm not backpedaling here…he's as real as the day is long, but I don't want to just leave you with that. So I'll leave you with this. I just heard a message the other day where the pastor practically belabored the point that "the promises of God are exceedingly great and precious." And that one of the very best promises goes like this: *God will never leave you.* Our God, who is Love, will never leave you. So, really, and I mean this… *really*…we have no need to fear because whatever comes our way, God will never leave us. And that's about all I can hope for this family and for yours and for mine.

V

Once upon a time, there was a girl who...

...embraced change and felt God...

Chapter 37

Ready and Willing, but Scared Out of My Mind

I'D BEEN HOPING to get to Africa. God had engaged my heart and my mind through some twisty life circumstances that left me broken and laid wide open for something new to come in. And Africa is what He decided to place inside me. I wanted to go on some kind of strategic trip that would help my church figure out a proper response to the AIDS crisis. Well, the summer had come and gone and Africa did not get stamped onto my passport. However, I was invited by Samaritan's Purse to attend a Pastors' Conference on HIV/AIDS in Haiti, and I actually said yes! Little Miss Diva said yes.

That trip was a gift on so many levels. First of all, it was basically tailor-made…it took place over the summer so my husband could be home with the kids, it was quick (just four days), it was a great taste of what Samaritan's Purse is doing in an area that our church is already involved in, it was close-ish (compared to a day and a half of travel to Africa), and it provided me with a cultural experience that my life sorely needed to put things into perspective, among other things.

Also, and this was hands-down the biggest lesson learned, I now know that I'm not the kind of person to let fear stop me. At the time of my trip, it was touted as the third most dangerous place to travel *in the world* and I'll be honest, I was downright scared that something was going to happen to me. When I told my husband, Kevin, a few days before I left that I had written a few letters to some people telling them

I love them and such for him to send out if I didn't come back, he said, "If you're that scared of something bad happening, then why are you going?" I said, interestingly without a second thought, "Because I need to prove to God and to myself that even though I really don't know if He'll protect me physically, I'll still do what I feel He's leading me to do."

I didn't think I had it in me, to tell you the truth. I felt pursued in this trip…this huge gift of a scary trip. Because sometimes, even in just the trying, even in just the act of being willing, and especially in the going, light breaks in. I felt pursued, so I felt compelled. And that's one lesson worth waiting for. So, what are you waiting for?

Chapter 38

No More Boundaries

LIFE IS ODD. Thirty or so hours ago I was eating breakfast in Haiti, and right now I'm taking a break from packing as we're moving to a new home this week.

The landscape of Haiti is simply stunning with towering mountains, flowering trees, and sweeping views of the ocean. However, what I saw on the hour-long car ride between the airport in Port-au-Prince and the conference location was simply unreal to me. It was as if I had driven through a National Geographic special. It's everything you see on TV, except I was seeing it all up close. The poverty is so real...I had to hold back tears several times. I couldn't get over the vast numbers of people, many just standing or sitting around (who doesn't want somewhere to go and something to do?). The purposelessness and monotony of their lives really struck me. So many thoughts ran through my head—why was I "destined" for such a cushy life in the States? Children really do bathe in and drink out of mud puddles. How even though I was immediately homesick when I arrived, I couldn't get past the impression that I felt God had followed me to Haiti and was whispering, "you are exactly where you're supposed to be right now."

On our last day, we visited an orphanage that my church supports. The beauty of the children took my breath away. They have the most gorgeous eyes and the darkest skin I've ever seen. Absolutely beautiful.

To hear one child after another whisper "bon soir" as they brushed my cheek with a kiss was almost more than I could bear.

Another realization was something I wrote in my journal one morning while sitting on a Haitian beach watching the sun come up... "A year ago, had anyone told me that I'd be observing an AIDS conference, let alone in Haiti, basically by myself, I would've thought they were out of their minds. This was not even on my radar one year ago. Further proof that following You is an adventure and no one can predict where You'll lead a willing heart."

My passion, as I anticipated, to do something—*anything*—to help people in a third-world country skyrocketed, as I bet God had planned. My prayer as I was flying home was this: "I hope I don't forget all I've seen, and that what I saw is how two-thirds of the world lives. Two-thirds live in unimaginable poverty. *They* are not the minority—*I am*. Don't let me forget, Jesus. Don't let me forget..."

But I also walked away with one final thought...I can do anything through Christ, anything He ever wants me to do...there are no boundaries now.

In each season of life there are limits. But no matter our limits, if God calls, He'll break down those barriers. I was terrified to go—Haiti is a dangerous place—and before I left, I wrote letters to my kids saying goodbye. Life is too short to not do what God wants you to do...it's too short to wait for the next season of life to usher in supposed-just-out-of-reach freedom. With God, all things are possible. If He's leading you...in any area...follow Him with all your heart. Let Him love you in the scary places. Let Him show you exactly where He wants you to be, and He'll take care of the rest.

Chapter 39

Things Change, God Doesn't

LIFE IS FUNNY. Things can change on a dime. Things can change that you never would have predicted could change. I have been highly allergic to cats and dogs for well over twenty years. My kids have begged for a pet regardless of that pertinent fact and I have stood strong with a firm "no" each and every time it came up. I wasn't trying to be mean, I just knew my life would be miserable if we had a pet living in our home. If you had told me yesterday morning that by the end of the day today I would be a cat owner, I would've thought you were crazy. But things can change and life is funny that way. Because today I found myself driving home with the cutest little kitten sitting right there on my lap. My husband wanted a "farm cat" to help keep the mouse population down at our new home now that we have some extra land. And I actually said yes. What I said yes to and what we got were two very different things, though. But isn't that just like life, too? I said yes to a grown-up outdoor uncute cat. Not a sweet, defenseless, how-could-I-ever-let-it-sleep-outside just-too-cute-for-words kitten. Things change. Opinions can change.

A month ago, I intentionally began the process of softening my heart toward someone. I invested into this person in a way that I hadn't in a long time. I was deliberate. I was kinder. And I went into it with the thought that the other person might not change at all in response to me, might not even notice the changes I was trying to make, and that would be okay. Had you told me one month before that I would be kicking down the self-imposed boundaries I had erected over the years, I would have thought you were crazy. But things can change, and life is funny that way. What I started out trying to accomplish and what has come out of it are two different things. Because what has been happening in me is not only a softening, but a strengthening as well. A new (somehow) ability to not need to be in control, to not know what someone is going to do with the emotional freedom I give them. Things change. Hearts can change.

About a year ago, I met with two friends a day apart and we had two separate yet mysteriously similar conversations. A fire had started in me regarding AIDS and Africa that led to my husband and me seriously considering adopting internationally. We spent a few months praying about it, with me reading everything I could get my hands on. One night while reading, I put down the book, and said out loud to God, "If there's a little girl over there (in Africa) that You want me to go get, I will." I shared this with these two friends for prayer support and wisdom, and they both told me that they and their husbands were also considering international adoption. God was doing something in us together, separately, and we were blown away. Fast-forward one year. One friend is not adopting, but she has become fully entrenched in the life of a refugee family from Burundi, Africa as she helps them with all the daily and monumental tasks of adjusting to life in North America; and she loves it, telling me just the other day that she has found her "thing" in this. My other friend and her husband have adopted a little girl from Ethiopia, a beautiful little girl. And we anxiously awaited her arrival and welcomed her with open arms when she came. My husband and I are not adopting, but we had the privilege and great blessing of contributing financially to our friends' adoption. Along with that, I spent a few days in Haiti last summer, went to Sierra Leone nine months later, and have new plans to go to Liberia in the summer all because of this new passion in me. Had you told us a year ago that my friend would be driving Burundis to doctors' appointments and taking them grocery shopping, and my other friend would be adopting a little girl from the heart of Africa, and that I'd be a key part in an African girl's adoption as well as visiting third-world countries (more than one!) sometime over the next year or two, well, we all would have thought you were crazy. But things can change and life is funny that way.

What I prayed for, hoped for—another little girl of my own with dark, dark skin and another language to decipher living under my roof and what has come out of those prayers and hopes are two very different things. But God responds to our hearts' cries in beautiful ways…He brings us along, He shapes our experiences, which in turn shape what we hope for, and then He creates these interwoven tapestries that are breathtaking, and far more meaningful and redemptive than where our prayers and wishes first started. Things change. People can change.

So here's what I keep learning, over and over and over again—to wait on God passionately and expectantly. What you think your year is going to look like, or your month, or this day, could up-end itself in a breath. (And I have a kitten to prove it.) But hold on tight, because God never, ever changes. God remains faithful through it all. Life is funny and amazing and beautiful that way.

Chapter 40

Slowing to a Stop

I'VE BEEN THINKING a lot about moving more slowly. How I run through my days. How I've been running through my kids' childhoods. (In nine years, they won't be living with me anymore. *Nine years...*) How Jesus lovingly calls us to give Him our burdens and in exchange He will give us rest. To quote an author friend of mine, Keri Kent, Jesus never said to us, "Get over here! I have a lot for you to do!" I laughed loudly when I heard her say that. Maybe because it resonated so deeply. Maybe because deep down I've actually thought that. A good Christian woman serves God. That's what we're supposed to do. Sure. But are we supposed to run ourselves into the ground? Do I want my children, my daughter especially, equating ministry with exhaustion and meetings and tasks that don't really fit?

I had the privilege of going away on a personal retreat for two days right after the new year started. I love doing that annually to look back over the past year...you know, take stock. I spent the first day reading my journals from the past fifteen months. If you're not a journal writer or even only a sporadic one, no big deal, right? But if you're like me, a fairly faithful everyday journal keeper, well, then that's another story. It took me nine hours to read them (and I knew how everything was going to turn out!). And when I was finished, I had a headache and I was depressed. And why was that? Because a few themes bubbled to the surface in that marathon reflection. One, the number of times that I complained about something in my life gave me pause...okay, to be more honest, I was ashamed; because I am really, really blessed. And two, the number of times I said something like, "I'm low energy this morning" or "wish I could stay here on the couch in my jammies today...that's not gonna happen for another week or so" were innumerable. And it made me sad. It made me sad to think that I'd filled this past year of my life with activities, many of them apparently ones I don't enjoy, that I don't find fulfilling, that just don't fit me or my introverted personality or my season of life. I've been running. But for what? And for who?

If I think I'm doing all of this to please God, well, I think I've got another thing coming. Because to be truthful, I don't know the last time really that I handed God my day or my agenda and just asked Him what He wanted me to be doing. I've been doing what I've been doing for years now and I think it's starting to hit me that what I'm doing and who I'm wanting to be just aren't the same things anymore. I've been round-hole/square-pegging it for a while. Longer than I want to admit. Longer than I may even know.

So I'm working through some questions with God, because I want His input this time around. Should I keep on doing and doing and doing, or can I stop? Is that allowed? Is that doable? And if I just stopped for awhile, even a long while, what would that mean, what would that look like, and dare I ask what's really deep down—what would other people and God think of me? Who just *stops*? Who isn't busy? No one I know. But I'm letting myself realize and remember that God called me to an abundant, free, joyful life, not a packed-out, constricting, complain-y, busy one full of activities that I just endure and that more than I'd like to admit actually make me cringe. And—this is the best part—bottom line, my heavenly Father's going to love me no matter what. Even if I stop.

Anything you and God need to take stock of? Wondering if God will still love you if you don't fill-in-the-blank anymore? Think again.

Chapter 41

In My Rearview Mirror

A COUPLE MONTHS AGO I began tossing around the idea of slowing down, about maybe even stopping. So after outright asking God if I could quit my job and Him gently assuring me that it would be okay, that all would be well, that He would still love me, I stopped. I quit my job of four-and-a-half years, at the church I've attended for fifteen years. I never thought I'd leave that job. I thought they'd have to wheel me out in about thirty years because I no longer understood "the younger generation." (To be honest, I still don't have a firm grasp on what *post-modernism* means, so I guess I was one foot out the door already.) This stepping down stunned even me. I'm still in process over the implications as, at the time of this writing, I've only been out of work and back from Africa for a few weeks. But I can already feel the relief settling into my bones.

I have to admit though that I'm scared. Will I fill my time with television and shopping? Will I become more isolated without the requisite meetings filling up my life? Will I pursue God and what I think I hear He's calling me to? Which is still blurry at best... Something about resting. And listening. And following my passion. But beyond that it's just people resembling walking trees. Sorry, random Mark 8 reference...in other words, my future is not yet all that clear, to say the least. Which in and of itself is scary.

A few years ago I remember being on a walk in my cuter-than-cute neighborhood. And I remember wondering how God would ever be able to inject surprise and adventure into my pretty darn set-in-place life. I knew who my husband would be for the rest of my life. I knew who my two children would be for the rest of my life. I knew the house I would grow old in and the streets I'd try to defy aging on by walking up and down them. I knew the church I'd marry my kids off in. I knew the job I'd have to be carted away from. I knew the five girls who'd be my closest friends til my dying day. My only future travel would entail the occasional trip to California and Las Vegas to visit with family. I knew my passion would be encouraging women and my hobbies would be writing and speaking. I was all set in stone, thank you very much. And quite happily, I might add.

And now…just a short couple years later, I live in a different house on a plot of land that doesn't even sit in an actual neighborhood, my church has changed identity and pastors, my passion is for the heart of the poor and a continent I finally got to experience firsthand, I've been to two third-world countries, and my job is in my rearview mirror. The husband, kids, and friends stay standing, though one has moved away and there are a few new ones on the list that I never would have expected, which I'm grateful for… though even each of those relationships are growing, changing, shifting a bit as time marches on. But man, oh, man. Did I ask for all this upheaval? I don't think so. It's been so much in so little time. The human part of my soul whispers, "It's been too much, Jesus…please stop for a little while…I can't handle any more change…" But the resilient part, the divine part, says just a bit louder, though still in a whisper, "Here we go…slow me down, heal me up, then what's just up ahead? I can take it…"

You know what? I can only hear that quiet deep down Voice because I'm choosing to throw off some of my hindering things. And this is just the beginning. There were so many times I hushed that Voice along the way because of my busyness. But not anymore. I'm going to walk slower and breathe more deeply and sit a bit longer with that cup of tea and listen, really listen, to the still small, thankfully persistent voice of God. "Be still and know that I am God," (Psalm 46:10 NIV). And I cannot wait to discover what surprises and adventures are just around the bend for this tired but hopeful girl.

Are you quiet enough to hear the Voice of the One who's trying to whisper of His love?

Chapter 42

Let Us Return

A FEW YEARS AGO, I was depressed. Something really bad had happened to someone I cared about deeply and it completely threw me. Reorganized my faith. Six months had gone by, and the darkness hadn't fully lifted. I was moving forward, I was choosing to no longer be irreverent in my healing, but I was still not me.

But then I went away on what would become my first of several retreats. God accompanied me on this getaway and I wrote the following in my journal about fifteen minutes after I arrived at the retreat center. It's basically a conversation that I had with God…and let me just say, I didn't hear an audible voice booming from the clouds, which is what we Christians always say so people don't think we're loco…but He spoke to me in my heart so clearly and so exactly what I needed to hear, that I have no doubt that God's Spirit was speaking to my spirit:

God: Do you believe I exist?
Beth: Yes, of course I do. How could I not? Look at all this beauty—this is no accident.
G: So, what is it then? Do you think I don't love (_____)? And that I therefore don't love you? And that I won't protect you since I didn't protect her?

B: Jumping right in, are we? No, I know You love her. And I know You love me. But I no longer think You'll protect me. I think I used to think I would have an extra measure of protection because I was Yours.

G: *You do and you don't. There are some things I will keep you from just because you are mine. But there are some things I won't.*

B: The past six months, I have been loving only the part of You that I understood. I haven't given You all of my heart because I haven't been trusting You completely.

G: *There are things you won't understand and can't understand. My ways are higher than your ways. Besides, if I were completely understandable, what kind of God would I be?*

B: So You're saying that You are calling on me to love You, trust You, obey You, and worship You, even though I can't fully understand You.

G: *Yes. And in exchange, I can promise you this:*
I will love you every day for the rest of your life and into eternity,
I will be with you every day for the rest of your life and into eternity,
and I will not stop transforming you into the likeness of Christ until the transformation is complete.

I sat there for a minute, soaking in the reality that God had just generously bent down to bring me healing; and I wiped some tears away. As I stood up, I picked up one of those little helicopter leaves, you know, the seed of a silver maple tree…there were two stuck together. I had never seen two stuck together like that before in my life. But I picked it up and said, *this side will remind me to trust You for the things I understand, and this one will remind me to trust You for the things I don't.* (I actually brought several of those little double helicopters home and to this day have them placed throughout my home to remind me of that promise I made to God.)

My faith has never been the same since. The darkness of doubt was lifted off me in that moment and I felt a gentle peace. God graciously granted me a fresh start.

Let Us Return

Come, let us return to the LORD. He has torn us to pieces but He will heal us; He has injured us but He will bind up our wounds. After two days He will revive us; on the third day He will restore us, that we may live in His presence. Let us acknowledge the LORD; let us press on to acknowledge Him. As surely as the sun rises, He will appear; He will come to us like the winter rains, like the spring rains that water the earth.

—Hosea 6:1-3 (NIV)

Chapter 43

Will the Real Church Please Stand Up?

I WANT TO TELL you about my church. The church I used to go to. I think I maybe exalted it to a place higher than church is supposed to be. I'm not sure even Acts 2 believers felt about their church what I felt about my church. My husband and I first attended there two weekends after our wedding. The first church we looked at together as a couple. We went back every weekend since. And every Wednesday. And every potluck dinner. We didn't look any further. We just knew that it was the church for us.

There is an irony in the lack of depth of how I chose it as our first place to check out. I had driven by it several times and thought, "What a cute little white church." That's it. That is the entire foundation to which fifteen years of commitment stands. I thought it was *cute*. (Well, that's how Kevin picked *me*, and look at us fifteen years later…)

But the weekends melted into years. I got baptized there (though I had been a believer for about ten years already). We became members there. I got my first job after marriage there, becoming their first official church administrator (second only to the pastor's wife who did the job out of their home a few hours a week). I watched my boss, our pastor, get kicked out of his position there due to a breach in what he said he wouldn't say from the pulpit that he ended up saying. We had our daughter there, and dedicated her there. I started the Women's Ministry there. We had our son there, and dedicated him there. I gave the Mother's

Day message there (the last one of its kind as women were no longer allowed to preach after me…not because I sucked, but because of a change in policy…at least, that's what I was told). I struggled hard with their stance on women in leadership there. (When we first began attending, there was a woman on their "advisory council." I misunderstood that to mean they would have women elders when the time came to transition that council to an official elder board. I was mistaken.) I laid that argument of mine down there…not changing what I believed but choosing to not die on that hill.

I met several of my closest friends there. I was asked to be on staff over communications, connections, and small groups there, taking on my first real grown-up job (the other position was a secretary, plain and simple, and just wasn't "me"). We watched a friend grieve the death of her young husband there. We gave large amounts of money to further the Kingdom there. I fought with people there who didn't like me. One time, a gal whom I'd known for maybe ten years, handed me a letter with a list of my faults that she had compiled from several unnamed sources, just as a heads up…something she thought I might want to know about and maybe, I don't know, work on fixing. But you know what? Even *that* was Church. That I didn't slap her was Church. That I thought about it but didn't was Church. That we actually talked it through was Church. I also fought with people there who loved me completely. I baptized my mom there. I picked out my kids' future spouses there. I laughed there, I cried there, I worshiped there, I served there. I lived and breathed there. It was my second home, my extended family. We were never going to leave. We were going to grow old there.

But then something changed. My pastor and his wife left, as pastors and their wives sometimes do. And I could barely handle it. Because for six years, not only had those two become two of my closest friends, but we were all onto something, those of us in leadership. We took each hill together, time and again. We were a part of something bigger than just us. We were trying new things, reaching new people, praying, struggling, celebrating, loving being together and getting to do this thing with each other. But they left. And then, well, then we were adopted by a church ten times our size.

I was at the front lines of lobbying for this adoption to come to pass. I had always wanted to work for a "big church" and what were our options? Hire another guy who would probably get burned out like the last guy? Or try something really different. It had seemed as if God's hand were in it. What were the odds of us losing and needing a pastor, and this other entity looking for a location to start a new campus in our neck of the woods, and oh yeah, they had a guy who'd be our pastor? Those were God odds.

So the vote passed. Ninety-one percent or something like that of the membership voted yes. And we became one of three campuses of a mega-church. The red-headed stepchild, as I've heard us called. Because things were bumpy and feelings were stepped on and not considered from time to time. It didn't feel like we were all taking hills anymore. Hills were taken by the staff and then we were told about them in an upfront verbal announcement and then we all clapped to celebrate what "we" and God had apparently accomplished.

Change is hard. I said those three words a thousand times in the months to follow, when someone would ask how the transition was going. What else could I say? *Well, my church has died and the remains have been eaten up by a bigger, meaner church without feelings apparently, but other than that, aces.* No one needed to know that was how I felt. First of all, I was on staff and needed to lead the way in transitioning healthily. I needed to be a cheerleader. Only problem, I couldn't find my pompoms to save my life. Besides, truthfully, that was just how *I* felt. And with how close I was to our former pastor and his wife, and with how in the loop I had been for so many years, I had a unique view. A view that, I have a feeling, few others shared with me. Or at least didn't share it to the same level of intensity that I did. Which is probably good.

So now, I am months past quitting my job. I am not there each time the doors are open. In fact, I even turned in the keys that I had on my keychain for fourteen years. I just go there now. On Sundays and that's it. I don't even serve. (Not yet, at least.) And we're trying to decide if we're staying. My sweet little church is dead. I go to a different church now. I mean, it's in the same building, but it might as well be in another state, another country, it's so different. Some people have left, although most have stayed. Our pastor is thirteen feet tall (we get him on a big screen, with a message that the "main campus" gets the week prior). They even painted the exterior of the building a vaguely tan color…so much for it being cute and white. I just go. And I walk in, get my weekly welcome, sit through the service, and on some Sundays, get my kids and walk right out. I don't do small talk, and even if I did, there isn't the pull to stick around long after a service like there used to be. For better or worse, with no doing or undoing on my part, I am becoming increasingly disentangled with this community and this place. Everything's different and it makes me so sad even to pull up there sometimes. Sara Groves sings, "I don't want to leave here…I don't want to stay…seems like pinching to me…either way…" Sing it, sister.

Will we stay or will we go? I have no idea. All I know today as I randomly grieve the passing of my beloved church is that I'm having a girls' night at my house this evening, and two of the eight women are from the "other" campus, which means had we not gone through all this, I wouldn't even know them. So that's my attempt to celebrate the crumbs even though the loaf of bread has been eaten all up.

A few months later…

I think there may be a chance that I have been living in the past. Holding on a bit too tightly. What we had, as a church family, way back then was something special. I've spoken to a few others who said it was unlike any other church experience they had before or since. And it is a time filled with wonderful memories for me. When my church was my second home. When I couldn't imagine being anywhere else than with those people. When I considered those people my real family. But seasons come and go. I don't feel that way about my church anymore. I don't work there anymore. We don't have a midweek service anymore, so I'm there on Sunday mornings and the occasional extra event, that I now choose to go to or not go to as opposed to having to be there because of my staff status or wanting to be there because why would I be anywhere else?

The few people who knew we were tossing around the idea, not lightly, of staying or not staying have asked what made us finally decide to stay. And there are multiple reasons. Everything from the great book *Life After Church* by Brian Sanders that helped me process all the entangled emotions to not wanting to add another change to my kids' lives on top of a new home and new school and new friends. But I think the main reason is history. We have a history there that rivals the best and worst of any family. I love that I know that K. married M. after the accident. I love that I know that P. has a Glamour Shots picture of herself. I love that I know that F. was actually dating H.'s babysitter when they first met. I love that I know that D. used to steal things. I love that I know that B. is one of the most actual grown-up people I know and yet he blows bubbles in church. (*Love* that.) I love that I know that R. loves animals almost more than people. I love that I know that S. is in recovery and N. doesn't like me very much and T. wants to be a pastor someday and that my kids took their first steps and said their first words among these people and that policies and staff and bricks and mortar and paint color may change but people, even if they come and go, even if they don't always like each other a whole lot, hold something for each other that can't be replaced or recreated by going to the church down the street. I have been loved well here and that's worth holding on to.

So now I just go. And I'm learning to serve again, a little at a time. And you know what? It's really okay. Because I am still loved here. It may not by the same. But it's really, really okay.

And even later still…

I don't want to end on this note. I don't want to give the wrong impression. First of all, the whole way through this process I met some incredible people that I never would have met had we stayed our cute, little, white church. Incredible people. People I have learned so much from, people I have laughed so hard with.

And secondly, I have had some of the most provocative experiences since the adoption…mainly Haiti, Sierra Leone, Open Door Clinic, the AIDS Task Force, and Liberia. Experiences that would not have been afforded me without our attachment to a big church. To this big church.

So, change is hard. But it can be good. This one has been both. And I see God's loving hand all over the change and all throughout the people.

Chapter 44

Don't Give Up. Ever.

THIS IS ONE of my favorite stories. Okay, this one technically is two stories for the price of one. Lucky reader…and you thought you were just getting one essay.

I grew up believing in Jesus. Believing He was the Son of God. Believing He died on the cross for our sins. Going to church. Singing "Jesus Loves Me" every single night. But something was missing. I couldn't put my finger on it. But one night when I was fifteen, I wrote a poem/letter to God. I told God that I wanted to be closer to Him, and that I was sorry I didn't try hard enough or read the Bible or spend time with Him, but that I would work on it. Starting right then.

I picked up my Precious Moments® Bible and began reading in Genesis. I fell asleep around Genesis 4. And felt terribly guilty. But about a week or so later, I was invited to this place called the Christian Youth Center. I'll be honest…there were rumblings that it was a cult. Jesus freaks went there on Tuesday and Friday nights. But I thought, *what the heck…a chance to meet cute boys.* (I was so very deep back then.) So, on Tuesday, February 4, 1986, I went. And that night someone explained to me that Jesus didn't die on the cross for the generic sins of the world, but for *my* sin.

Truth be told, that was a bit of a hump for me to get over. I didn't consider myself a sinner. I was a good kid. Like, pathetically good. Like I grounded myself when I didn't make the honor roll. (I so wish I were kidding.) But it didn't take them long to convince me obviously because that very night I accepted Christ as my Savior. My real life started that night. Jesus had been waiting for that night. I got in the car with my stepdad when he picked us up, and after he had dropped off my two friends, I looked at him and said, "Why didn't anyone ever tell me this?!" He thought I was nuts, I'm sure. (That was the first story...but watch how I weave it seamlessly into the second story.)

Though I grew up religious, per se, my parents weren't followers of Christ as I had come to wake up to. (This is kind of funny—I remember that when people would ask me what I "was," I would answer that I was a Protestant Republican. Like when I was eight. I guess I figured that pretty much covered it.) So, me coming home talking about Jesus, what I can only imagine as constantly, had to throw my mom and stepdad for a loop. Especially as I was a teenager, who, though a goody two-shoes, still had some faults. I remember my mom saying something like, "How can you call yourself a Christian and not vacuum?!" To which I would mutter under my breath, "Because I'm still a teenager who hates to vacuum!" and lift my feet onto the coffee table to unselfishly get out of her way. Then I would turn up the volume on "All My Children." *That* was Christian of me...

We suffered through the rest of my teenage years, and I moved out to go to college. I prayed for the salvation of my parents (all of them) for years, but, I hate to admit, not with a ton of intensity. I think a part of me just thought, *Okay, they know what they need to do, I've said everything I can, now God needs to send someone else into their lives to talk them through it because they've had it up to here with me yappin' about it.*

Along the way, I'd send up the occasional plea on their behalf, usually after an especially convicting sermon. When we were getting ready to start construction on our addition to our church building, our pastor had us all take those little boundary flags and write names of people on them who we hoped to bring to Christ in that new building. I wrote down my mom's name.

One day, eighteen years after I became a Christian, I found myself at a conference that I did not want to be at. It was a Baptist thing, not that I have anything against Baptists, but I was expecting to be bored out of my mind (and I was) and had so many other things I just knew

I could be doing. Then the last speaker took the stage and floored each and every one of us. Yes, at a Baptist convention. He was an ex-convict and I'm forgetting every detail of his story except one line…in telling how he came to Christ, he said that his mother had "sent Jesus after him" and that Jesus had taken her up on it. So that week, I apologized to Jesus for not praying more fervently for my family and friends that I cared about, and I sent Jesus after them.

Later that week, I got an e-mail from my mom saying, basically, that she had given her life to Christ. Eighteen years of praying. Eighteen years of waiting. I am so glad I didn't give up on her. Or God.

Six months later, I had the privilege of participating in, hands down, one of my top ten best life moments when I baptized my mom in our new church building, and later that day, I handed her the flag that had her name written on it.

Don't give up, don't give up, don't give up. If you're just hanging on, if you feel you're simply prayed out, if you're wondering if God is even hearing you, don't give up. Because God still answers prayer. He loves to do that for us. And He still saves.

Chapter 45

Spring of the Soul ✐

SPRING IS FINALLY arriving. My yard is turning a beautiful shade of green. So is my soul. It is spring in my soul. It's been a long winter. And I'm not just talking about Illinois.

My husband and I went through a seventeen month crisis. Then we went through the change-y-ist year of our lives (friends moving away, church being adopted, moving to a new home in a different town, et cetera, et cetera). Then I quit my job, went to Africa, cut my hair, was dealt an emotional blow to the gut, and then somehow...*somehow*... the thaw has set in. Already. *Thank You, Jesus.* Like I said, it's been a long winter.

I am so very tired. So tired that I didn't know I was tired. Ever been there? God is granting me so much rest, I feel like a kid in a candy store. (Or, in my case, an adult in a candy store...I have an unhealthy and inappropriate-for-my-age love of all things candy.) But really, I feel like I'm being led beside quiet waters.

I am hurting. Deep in my soul hurting. God is pouring peace and comfort and grace into my soul in really sweet, intimate ways. This part hasn't come easy. This part has been a battle. This part is not being handed to me...I'm having to work for it. I'm having to fight against false accusations that my enemy wants me to believe, but I'm saying, "Nope, not this time." And not to sound cocky, because that can be very dangerous, but right now, I'm winning. In other words, I'm feeling myself being healed. I'm feeling myself waking up. I'm aware of His Presence.

I am scared. Okay, maybe scared isn't quite the right word. I was thinking I'd walk into this job-less season of life without a purpose. With people judging me and asking, "So, what do you actually fill your days with now that you're not working?" And some people have. And I've smiled each time and said, "So far, nothing." Though that's not completely true, there's been a freedom in proclaiming that with confidence and a sick delight in seeing them squirm. Okay, so if I haven't been scared…what is it then? Well, maybe not a *fear* of being purposeless. I think I perhaps *have been* purposeless. For awhile now. Oh, I just figured it out. It's not purposelessness. I've been multi-purposeful. And that sometimes is worse. I've been running in a bunch of directions. But now I've got time and space to simply ask God, "What's up for today?"

(Side note: Just this morning, in the fog of waking up, I asked Him, "What do You want me to do this summer?" It's April 15…I'm not sure why I asked Him that. Nothing came to mind, so I moved on. About eight hours later I got an e-mail of a very, very, very potential one-person trip back to Africa *this summer* to do some reconnaissance. (Okay, it's not really reconnaissance, but I love that word and was pleasantly surprised to see that I spelled it right on the first go round.) Now, it may not at all come to pass…but how intimate and quirky of God was that? Love Him!)

And here's what's been up for today, for the past couple of todays… I've been writing like a banshee. Not that banshees write. What exactly is a banshee anyway? All I recall is that they're known for their screaming, not their writing. I just looked it up…that is not at all the analogy I want to leave you with here. So let's just say, I'm writing like I maybe have never written before. Purpose is clarifying for me.

And I'm learning, maybe for the first time in my life, to be okay with having nothing to do. To have no guilt attached to it. The other day at breakfast, my daughter was praying, "God, help Daddy have a good day at work, help Jack and me have a good day at school, and help Mommy have a good day at home doing nothing again…oh, wait, do you have Pilates?…okay, help Mommy have a good time at Pilates and *then* a good day at home doing nothing again." Can I just say, rest is delicious and up to this point in my life, I'd been consuming it in hors d'oeuvres-size bites, but now…now I'm stepping up to the banquet and am delighting in what I'm seeing and binge-eating my way through.

I slowed to a stop, and I was scared to…not completely sure God was leading in this or I was just ticked off with my circumstances. Not sure I'd be loved in the stopping. But it turns out that this is *exactly* where He wants me. Spring's here.

Afterword

OKAY, HERE'S THE real reason I wrote this book. I couldn't *not* write it. Let me try to explain. I am going through a hard time (well, at this writing I am…don't know if I still am by the time you're reading it). And though, yes, Jesus loves me this I know, for the Bible tells me so, I am coming to realize so clearly that *my life* also tells me so. My life is one story after another of God showing up. Of God being faithful beyond measure. Of God pursuing me intimately. Of God engaging in the details of my life. Of God living out His eternal commitment to me. And God, in His graciousness, wisdom, and intimate love for me, kept bringing one story after another to my mind.

Ummm, Beth, remember how you couldn't eat most foods? I healed you and still do and still will.

Pssst, Beth, remember the time I told you where to find the wallpaper border? I talked to you…like really talked to you…and still do and still will.

Hey, Beth, remember when I came through on that new, better job for Kevin, just in the nick of time? I provided for you…when you needed it…I still am above time and still do come through.

Wow, Ms. Short-Term Memory Girl, remember the time I saved your mom after you prayed for her for eighteen years? I saved her…I listened to your prayers…I answered them…and still do and still will.

My life has been, and I hope will continue to be, a combination of hard, funny, and sweet moments. I need reminding that God is the Author and Finisher of my faith. The Author and Finisher of my moments. The Author and Finisher of my stories. The Author and Finisher of my *entire life*. And He is yours too. If you'll let Him.

Be faithful. He'll be faithful back. Pursue Him. He's been pursuing you all along. Engage with Him. He engages with you from morning til night and can't wait until you wake up again the next day. Commit to Him. He is the most committed Partner you will ever hope to find. And this is what I know: He *is* just that into you.